West Academic Publishing's Emeritus Advisory Board

West Academic Publishing's Law School Advisory Board

a short & happy guide to
Mindfulness

Glen-Peter Ahlers, Sr.
Professor of Law
Barry University Dwayne O. Andreas School of Law

A SHORT & HAPPY GUIDE® SERIES

WEST ACADEMIC

860 Blue Gentian Road, Suite 350
Eagan, MN 55121
1-877-888-1330

Published in the United States of America

ISBN: 978-1-64242-088-3

To my six magnificent children, all adults whom I still refer to as my fuzz butts. You continue to delight and astound me as you find your way through life, and you remind me that while I am a teacher, I am a student as well.

I could not Love you more nor be more proud of you; you are all gifts that keep on giving.

—GPA, a.k.a. Dad

Preface

You hold in your hands an opportunity to learn ways to face the tremendous stress and pressure that being and becoming a lawyer entails. This book is an offshoot of my passion to introduce law students to what mindfulness is and to the positive benefits that practicing mindfulness can bring. The remarkable amount of stress practitioners face does not begin after passing the bar; the stress begins to invade your life at the beginning of your legal career, when you start learning the law. Stress comes with the legal profession. Learning how to deal with stress does not. Practicing mindfulness consists of simple, doable exercises that can help us manage "the complete catastrophe."

I searched for an on-off switch to my life for many years. The problem with what I envisioned, something like a light switch I could flip off when it was time for bed, was that it required a very trusted someone to flip the switch back on in the morning. I needed to find a solution that did not require someone else to switch the switch.

Growing up various solutions presented themselves, but none of them sufficed. Turns out that even sex, drugs, and rock n' roll have their limitations and too much of the last two could result in hangovers. (Sometimes did.)

Neither did growing my hair to the middle of my back, putting college on hold, or leaving New York for Albuquerque, New Mexico suffice. I knew no one there, had no job and no place to live, but nonetheless, a good buddy of mine and I headed west.

Wandering in the desert, something I've always known became clear to me. The closest I ever came to an effective on-off switch were the pauses I enjoyed as I hiked and camped in the mountains. That was true as I grew up in New York too. Once a month my Scout troop camped and once a month I felt torn leaving the mountains behind as we broke camp and headed home Sunday morning. I grew up in a loud, loving family, liked school, enjoyed good friends and even had one girlfriend throughout high school. Life was good! And yet one Sunday a month I felt a little torn to leave the mountains.

Decades passed and life continued as did my search for my switch until Eckhart Tolle's 1997 book *The Power of Now* came to my attention. Grabbed my attention. The simple elegance and wisdom of learning to focus on what was immediately before me instantly made infinite sense. I seized the message, and I ran with it. As I felt the benefits calm me, my interest in learning more about mindfulness grew like a fever. And then I realized that I was in an excellent position to introduce the message to my very stressed law students.

Research shows that law students suffer from higher levels of stress than all other postgraduate students. While you may not have known that, you probably are aware of classmates who turn to alcohol, drugs, and other unhealthy habits to try to alleviate the pressures of law school. This is a dangerous precedent. Successful lawyers need a solid understanding of the law and the ability to implement it. Our understanding of the law grows in time beginning in law school; our ability to implement our knowledge of the law depends upon our physical, mental, and emotional health. At a minimum, practice-ready lawyers must handle enormous amounts of stress without going off the rails.

What good is having a thorough understanding of the law if you cannot execute your acumen? What good are you to a prospective client if you can't focus on the intake interview because you haven't more than a couple of hours of sleep a night for several weeks? What good are you to your client, to your firm, and to the judicial system if you forget to timely file a motion because of too many late nights visiting the wrong bar? What good are you to your family if every minute not working is spent relaxing with more scotch and pills? What good are you to your spouse with whom you keep fighting because you are unhappy with yourself? What good are you to yourself if you cannot get going in the mornings because you are sad, depressed, demoralized, and unable to focus?

A balanced lifestyle helps keep the train on track. This requires that we balance proper diet, exercise, rest, and recreation along with work. While I believe practicing mindfulness would help all 8 billion people on earth, I think it is an especially terrific tool for those of us engaged in the legal profession. You have been at it long enough to realize that we are a stressed-out profession. The pressure and stress of practicing law does not wait until you are sworn in, it begins building during the first semester of law school.

Students in my three-day Mindfulness and the Practice of Law class often tell me how practicing mindfulness helped them. I include some of their (gently edited) statements to help illustrate the immediate impact felt by people who, like you, are walking around in I-want-to-be-a-lawyer shoes. Students like you who feel the stresses, strains, and tensions involved with navigating the minefield of life that incorporates family, friends, work, bills, health, and the law.

This book, like my one-credit course, can only introduce the concept of mindfulness and point out how regularly practicing it can make all the difference in the quality of life you enjoy moving forward. Mindfulness does not eradicate monthly bills, late financial aid checks, sudden medical issues, family emergencies, or any of the rest of the full catastrophe,[1] but it can help provide a little breathing room, a space for and a chance to choose responses instead of blindly reacting.

By Glen-Peter Ahlers, Sr.

November, 2023

---

[1] "I'm a man. So I married. Wife, children, house. Everything. The full catastrophe."—Zorba, from the film *Zorba the Greek* (1946, 20th Century Fox.)

Acknowledgments

I especially want to thank Jon Kabat-Zinn, Dave Potter, and the students in Mindfulness and the Practice of Law.

Jon Kabat-Zinn's excerpt of "dogness" from his seminal work *Full Catastrophe Living* appears with permission from the author and publisher, Penguin Random House LLC (US).

Dave Poter at Palouse Mindfulness (https://palousemindfulness.com/index.html) has graciously allowed me to include his headings regarding the content of his online MBSR course and to base my version of the guided Lake Meditation on the meditation he uses in the online course.

I would also like to thank the students who sat with me for three days to learn a little about Mindfulness. I appreciate their input, candor, and permission to anonymously include their experiences.

In today's rush we all think too much, seek too much, want too much and forget about the joy of just Being.—Eckhart Tolle

About the Author

A member of the faculty of Barry University's Dwayne O. Andreas School of Law in Orlando, Florida since 2002, Ahlers is a lifetime member of the Mindfulness in Law Society and a graduate of the Palouse Mindful-Based Stress Reduction course. Ahlers has helped coordinate, facilitate, and participate in mindfulness mini-conferences and other mindfulness-programming at the annual meetings of the Southeastern Association of Law Schools (SEALS) since 2018 and regularly provides local and regional presentations on the subject.

Ever searching for an "on-off button for life" that would allow moments of peace and pause in daily responsibilities, Professor Ahlers began earnestly practicing and researching mindfulness in the early 2000s after discovering Eckhart Tolle's 1997 book, *The Power of Now*. Recognizing the value of incorporating daily mindfulness activities into his own life, he tested student interest in learning about mindfulness when he first taught a one-credit "Practice Ready Institute" called Mindfulness and the Law in January 2018. The class proved so popular that he continues to teach it three times a year before the start of every semester.

After nearly 40 years of law library experience, over 30 of them as Director and Associate Dean, Professor Ahlers hung up his shooshing cleats and now teaches full time. During his library career he Served as President of Mid-America Law School Library Consortium, on the Board of Directors of the Consortium of Southeastern Law Libraries, as President of Mid-America Association of Law Libraries, two terms as President of the Southwestern Association of Law Libraries, as chair of the Association of American Law Schools Section on Law Libraries, as Scribes Executive Director, on the Arkansas Supreme Court Committee on Appellate Court Record Retention, on dozens of American Bar Association law school site teams, and as editor of numerous journals, newsletters, and blogs. Ahlers has also written, co-authored, and contributed to, and edited books on various topics.

Oh, and one last thing. Ahlers has an idiosyncrasy that we hope you do not take out on the editors; he capitalizes the word Love whenever he uses it. When queried, he replied that he did it to celebrate the bounty of Love in his life and to remind him of how simple and powerful the word is. "With Love everything is bearable, without it nothing is," he said.

Table of Contents

Preface v

Acknowledgments ix

About the Author xiii

Part 1. What Is Mindfulness? 1
What Mindfulness Is Not 5
Mindfulness Is Not a Way to Stop Our Thoughts 6
Mindfulness Is Not Hard to Practice 7
Mindfulness Is Not Easy to Practice 9
Mindfulness Is Not Just an Aspirin for the Mind 11
Mindfulness Is Not Complicated 12
Mindfulness Is Not a Destination 15
What Mindfulness Is 17
Paying Attention to What Is Presently Unfolding 17
Open Awareness of What Is Presently Unfolding 17
Acceptance of What Is Presently Unfolding 17
Not Identifying with What Is Presently Unfolding 18
Understanding You Always Have a Choice on How to Respond to What is Presently Unfolding 18
Buddha, Christ, Thoreau, and the Hippies 19
Experiencing Fully the Present Moment 21
The Five Senses 22
Movie Theater of the Mind 28
Mindfulness v. Mindlessness 33
Automatic Pilot 35
Autopilot Morning 35
Non-Autopilot Morning 36
Reasons for Not Autopiloting 41
Mindful Intentional Piloting and Mindless Autopiloting 45
Driving Past Our Exit 49
Giving Priority to Whatever Is Occurring in the Present Moment 50
MBSR 52
Non-Judging/Labeling 54
Beginner's Mind 55

Part 2. Why Practice Mindfulness? 57
Benefits of Practicing Mindfulness 57
Mindfulness Improves Focus 59

Practicing Mindfulness Reduces Anxiety and Increases Calm 61
Your Amygdala and Sabre-Toothed Tigers 62
Cell Phone and Internet Addictions 63
Because You Are Stressed out 67

Part 3. Practicing Mindfulness 71
Formal Meditation Practices 71
A Sitting Meditation Focusing on the Breath 72
Guided Meditations 76
MBSR's Lake Meditation 76
Professor Ahlers's Lake Meditation 78
Body Scans 83
Walking Meditations 87
Informal Practices 89
It's All About the Pause 89
Three Breaths 90
Incorporating Moments of Mindfulness Throughout the Day 90
Anytime, Anywhere 90
Using the Stairs 91
Washing Dishes 92
Brushing Your Teeth 93
Showering or Bathing 94
Enjoy a Glass of Water or Cup of Coffee or Tea 95
When Called on in Class 96
Stop Lights 97
Driving Without the Radio 97
Eating 98

Part 4. Additional Resources 101
People 101
Meditation Apps 103
Websites 104
Noteworthy Books 104
Noteworthy Blogs, Articles, and Reports 105

A Short & Happy Guide to Mindfulness

PART 1

What Is Mindfulness?

Mindfulness is an awareness that arises through paying attention, on purpose, in the present moment, non-judgmentally. —Jon Kabat-Zinn

The word 'mindfulness' has been bandied about long enough, that almost everyone has at least heard it. And everyone who has heard of mindfulness but who doesn't practice it, either has no idea what it is about or entertains some soggy-foggy notion of what it is all about. Many feel mindfulness is too far out there to be practical. In short, everyone has their own twist or misunderstanding of what mindfulness is, and it can be difficult to combine the myriad twists and interpretations into one consistent, coherent message. So, what, then, is all this mindfulness talk really about? When I talk about mindfulness, I mean Jon Kabat-Zinn's concept and definition of mindfulness: an "awareness that arises through paying attention, on purpose, in the present moment, non-judgmentally."

Oh great, you may be thinking, more gobbledygook! As if you don't already get enough gobbledygook in law school. But hold on. I help students wrap their heads around the Rule Against Perpetuities, one of the gobbledygookiest rules in law. Trust me, understanding mindfulness is easier than understanding the Rule Against Perpetuities. In fact, few things are simpler to explain than mindfulness. Being mindful—"the awareness that arises through paying attention" simply means paying attention to what is happening and unfolding in your presence at the moment—focusing on now instead of focusing on someone, someplace, something, or sometime else in the past or focusing on someone, someplace, something, or sometime else in the future. Learning what mindfulness is, may be easy, but practicing mindfulness, on the other hand, can be quite challenging.

If mindfulness is such a simple concept, you may ask, then why write a whole book about it? Well, for starters, my publishers would be disappointed if I just sent them a few paragraphs instead of a book manuscript. And I hope you, too, would be disappointed if I abruptly stopped here: "The End." What if, instead of opening *Moby Dick* with the immortal line "Call me Ishmael," Herman Melville told the story in two sentences? Perhaps "Captain Ahab was obsessed with killing a large, white whale. He failed. "The End". We certainly would not get the whole story, and we would be cheated out of one of the world's greatest books. Or, what if we shortened Will's play to one sentence? "Romeo and Juliet suffered a tragic Love." "The End." We wouldn't want to be cheated out of the immortal story, and I do not want to cheat you either, so I'll keep going.

I want to write the book to help introduce mindfulness to as many law students as I can. Because I feel learning to practice mindfulness is so important, I want to teach what I have learned about how practicing mindfulness techniques can help one remain calm, focused, and steady. I know firsthand how practicing mindfulness helps me in life, and my mindfulness students tell me how much it helps them. Have you ever rushed through a dinner?

(Burp!) Was your experience different than these takeout and home-cooked meals students shared with me?[1]

Takeout

> My mindful activity today was having dinner. It was a mindful experience because I ate my meal with focus. I even put my phone down and only focused on the food in front of me. I had takeout from one of my favorite restaurants and ate Kimchi wings, Tonkatsu Ramen, and Taro ice cream.
>
> The flavor of my wings was something I immediately noticed more. Before today, I'd swallow all six wings and move on. Today I took my time with each wing. I felt the crunchy texture and realized how much of a "kick" the kimchi gives them. Also, I only needed three wings instead of my usual six to feel satisfied!
>
> When it came to the ramen, it tasted so salty today. I don't know if it's usually this salty, and I never noticed, but I took my time with it, exploring the temperature and flavors of every little ingredient in the ramen. I could not finish it because, in the end, the salt flavor was too overpowering, and I moved on to my Taro ice cream.
>
> The ice cream was interesting, I didn't eat it super-fast like usual, so I didn't get any brain freeze like I tend to. Instead, I noticed how cold it was. A sensation I normally don't pay attention to. My mouth felt like it was freezing, and I was in pain; it made it very hard to just stay with it in my mouth. I usually don't take my time eating ice cream, so maybe that is why this is the first time I experienced this "cold" sensation.

---

1 All student work is included with permission.

Overall, I enjoyed my meal a lot more and was able to focus on ingredients and textures that now **I KNOW** I like or dislike for real. I've had this exact meal before on other occasions, but I never experienced it as I did today. Everything just seemed so different and heightened more than usual. Even the water I drank felt crisper. I felt how much more refreshed and hydrated I was afterward. I was able to eat with no distractions, and my overall mood was very positive throughout the whole experience.

Homecooked Tacos

I cooked and prepped 2 tacos with the following ingredients: beef with taco seasoning, lettuce, tomato, peppers, onions, hot sauce, and cheese.

First, I smelled the tacos before eating them. The smell of the hot sauce and the taco seasoning overpowered everything else.

I moved on to feeling the texture of the tortilla which was honestly not as soft as I would have liked. Maybe I should consider buying a different brand?

I took a small bite but did not chew so I could feel the textures of the ingredients inside the tacos. It was especially strange to feel the cool temperature of the lettuce compared to the hot meat and cheese.

I then began to chew slowly and felt the crunching of the lettuce, onions, and peppers, along with the gooey texture of the cheese. The main thing I tasted throughout was the seasoning mixed in with the beef.

My favorite part about eating slowly and mindfully was noticing all the various textures in the tacos.

Desserts taste better when eaten mindfully too. I don't know about you, but I am a bit of a Cookie Monster. Have you ever had a bag of cookies disappear and wonder where the cookies had gone?

Chocolate Chip Cookies

> Today I bought a box of chocolate chip cookies. Usually, I just eat a bunch of cookies as quickly as I can with no thought or regard. Today, after our lesson with the raisins, I decided not to just gulp the cookies down quickly. By slowing down, I actually enjoyed the cookies instead of hurriedly eating them. And I enjoyed a nice slowdown of my mind instead of the "go-go-go" I am used to. And another plus was that fewer cookies were consumed! Yay!

Paying attention to whatever we are doing at the moment allows us to truly experience what is going on instead of blindly plunging headlong into some future. Having dinner? Just have dinner. Spending time with a loved one? Just focus your attention on your loved one. Studying torts? Just study torts. Folding the laundry? Just fold the laundry. Studying Civ Pro? Just study Civ Pro.

When I expand and elaborate on what mindfulness means beyond Jon Kabat-Zinn's pithy definition, I often find it helpful to begin by explaining some things mindfulness is not. I find this helps untangle and slay some of the misconceptions people may have about what they think mindfulness is.

What Mindfulness Is Not

> *Mindfulness is not a mechanical process. It is developing a very gentle, kind, and creative awareness to the present moment.* —Amit Ray

Mindfulness Is Not a Way to Stop Our Thoughts

Practicing mindfulness doesn't stop our thoughts but can provide us pause and a space from which to view them with less attachment as if they were clouds floating through our mind's sky. Our minds are thought generators; incessant, perpetual, unrelenting thought generators. Think of the bubble machines or dancing blow-up figures you see on sidewalks trying to catch your attention as you drive by. Whether you think they are cute or annoying, they work, don't they? Our thoughts seek to grab our attention the same way. Thought after thought after thought, that's what our mind gives us. Dancing, waving, wriggling, incessant thoughts. We can't stop them. We would have better luck stopping the rising tide by digging our toes into the sand, holding outstretched palms toward the sea, and shouting, "Stop!" But stick with me; while practicing mindfulness does not stop the tide of our thoughts, it can help us seemingly slow down our thoughts or at least seemingly increase the space between them.

Practicing mindfulness does not change the rate of passing time, it just seems to. Our clocks, watches, phones, and computers still strike midnight at the appropriate time, but practicing mindfulness can help us retrain and improve our ability to focus on what is important in the present moment. Now I am going to let you in on a little secret. Most of the time, those incessant, perpetual, unrelenting, dancing, waving, wriggling thoughts are not what is most important in the present moment.

Think of your thoughts like the traffic that passes in front of you, left to right and right to left, as you wait at a red light. There is nowhere for you to go while the traffic passes through your vision. Explore the vehicles passing by, the big yellow plumber's truck, the little blue Audi, and the red convertible with Grandpa driving. See the silver minivans, the new and old Ford F150s, and the police cruiser—*glad he's going that way!*—the school bus, the tractor-trailer—*man, he's taking a wide turn*—and ooh, that Lamborghini! The red light stops you and pauses your commute, much the same way as practicing mindfulness pauses your automatic, unconsciously streaming commuting thoughts. As you wait at the light, you can watch the traffic cross your path without jumping into the driver's seat of any of the passing vehicles. You just let them drive by. (Although it would be nice to try out that Lamborghini!) The cars, trucks, and buses in all their hues pass in and out of your sight within seconds. Practicing mindfulness helps us cultivate the ability to let our thoughts go by like that. We notice our thoughts—we are happy about this, we are sad about that, we are tickled by this, angry she said that, and worried about final exams—but instead of dwelling on these thoughts, we let them pass without jumping into their driver's seat and suddenly taking off in a whole new direction. Unfortunately, most of us most of the time just jump from thought to thought, to thought, from vehicle to vehicle, to vehicle, without consciously thinking, and then we scratch our heads wondering how we wound up where we wound up. We unconsciously get lost in the traffic of our minds instead of paying attention to the route, to the purpose, to the commute we set out on.

Mindfulness doesn't help us stop our thoughts but helps us gain the ability to watch them pass by as we focus on what really matters, this present moment. Mindfulness helps us enhance our ability to focus on and pay attention to whatever we are immersed in. If we are studying property, mindfulness practice helps us focus on studying property. The incessant thought traffic of our minds doesn't cease; it merely continues with a lessened capacity for disrupting the present moment.

Mindfulness Is Not Hard to Practice

> *Mindfulness. . . is the very simple process of noticing new things, which puts us in the present and makes us more*

sensitive to context and perspective. It is the essence of engagement. —Ellen Langer

Mindfulness is not hard to practice. We cultivate mindfulness formally by setting a time each day to meditate and informally by participating in micro-meditations throughout the day. The formal and informal practices require no special equipment, no special shoes, no special workout attire, and no special gym. Each of us already has everything we need to practice mindfulness. And as we practice mindfulness, it begins to invite us to change lanes, take our foot off the thought-gas pedal, and perhaps even pull over to the side for a breather. (This may be tricky while driving on the Interstate, so be careful when, where, and how you employ mindfulness techniques.)

By formal practice, I mean setting a time, if not a time and a place, to meditate regularly. Like exercising, the more regular, the more betterer. A time to sit, as Andy Puddicombe, the founder of Headspace, says, "and do nothing." The more consistent the daily practice, the more effective the exercise is. The more consistent our informal micro-meditations, the more effective they will be as well. Think of formal and informal mindfulness exercises as an athlete views exercise. Athletes train daily. Not just when they feel like exercising. Not just when they have nothing else to do. Not just when the sun is shining or when the weather is perfect. Athletes know the power of consistent training. They train whether they want to or not. They train when they're tired. They train when they are hungry. They train because they have trained before and learned that keeping up with the training feels better than letting it go and having to start all over again to regain the strength, poise, and agility they are capable of.

Opportunities to practice micro-meditations are readily available. Every moment provides opportunities to practice. Whether you are farming, hiking, talking, studying, eating, showering, chasing the Cat in the Hat, or taking the cat to the vet, micro-mindfulness invites you to pause whatever the immediate activity is—even when answering your professor in class, or during your oral argument—to put down your mind's rake and hoe, and live in the moment. Enough practice helps you begin to develop a different sense of what is important, a sense of distance from your concerns, a sense of distance that minimizes anxieties and concerns—which, after all, are merely pesky, incessant, perpetual, unrelenting, dancing, waving, and wriggling thoughts that make themselves seem and feel important. Final exams are still coming, but they are not paramount anymore. Midterm exams are over and not worth worrying about (although they are always worth a review to see if there are ways to improve in the second half of the course.)

Mindfulness Is Not Easy to Practice

> *Instructing somebody to. . . release or dis-identify with his or her thoughts—is like trying to instruct somebody to instantly sneeze, or like telling someone just not to think, when the mind is built to do little else but that.* — Ira Israel

I know, I know, I know; I just said practicing Mindfulness is not hard. But I didn't say it was easy. Practicing mindfulness may seem easy—just sit and pay attention to the moment—but we are not used to just sitting and paying attention to our moments. As soon as we tell ourselves to just sit and pay attention to the moment, our minds begin to behave like a kindergartner's. *What do you mean, I have to sit still in my chair? I want to go over there and play with the blocks!* The idea of mindfulness is easy, but the practice is challenging. We may seem like we are sitting still, paying attention, but internally our minds are pinball-bouncing at light speed from one thought to another. This is frustrating as all get out to many beginning meditators who often think they are meditating wrong.

Mind racing is frustrating for experienced meditators from time to time as well, but we don't think we are meditating wrong. That's what meditation is—minds wandering off and coming back to the breath. Again. And again. And again. . . .

When we are at the gym lifting weights and our arms grow tired, we don't think, *oh, I must be lifting wrong*, because that's what lifting that much weight for that many repetitions feels like. When we are jogging, and our heart rate builds and our breath quickens we don't think, *oh, I must be jogging wrong,* because that's what jogging at that pace feels like. Our heartbeat and breath rate may hasten and we may feel our calves a bit more when we walk upstairs, but we don't think, *oh, I must be climbing the stairs wrong*. That's what taking the stairs feels like.

An intricate piano piece may seem easy for a concert pianist to play at Carnegie Hall, but it is not. The stamina, skill, and attention required to masterfully play is prodigious. I don't know about you, but for me, with my thousands of less hours of practice, it would not be easy. Likewise, the stamina, skill, and attention required of NASCAR drivers racing 500 miles in circles may be simple—keep turning left—but it is not easy. Ditto for the stamina, skill, and attention required of Olympic sprinters covering 100 meters; simple—run fast—but it is not easy. For most of us, our tuning-into-the-moment muscles are soft, if not atrophied from lack of use, but with time and training, we can build the muscles to better understand and face the joys and challenges life entails.

One of our greatest challenges today is glued to the palm of our hands. Because of our addiction to our ~~cellphones~~ portals-to-everywhere-but-here that are glued to our hands, it is far too easy for us to leave any moment and jump time and space to some other where, to some other when. Effortlessly and instantaneously we can transport ourselves to any other where, to any other when we choose.

Let's see, have I gotten a text in the last two minutes? I better check! And we're off to Chatland, wherever that is. We are no longer in the conversation we were having with our friend sitting in the booth opposite us. She's in that conversation alone, now in soliloquy, while we are hunting chats in Chatland. To be fair, our propensity to distraction was not instigated by the invention of palm-held portals-to-everywhere-but-here, but the portals do magnify and simplify our access to infinite and immediate distractions. I am amazed at how many students blindly cross campus staring into their own palms instead of enjoying Florida's Palms. It's a wonder they don't bump into things more often. It's almost as if they have downloaded a human version of Tesla's self-driving software, driverless people crisscrossing campus.[2]

Mindfulness Is Not Just an Aspirin for the Mind

> *Mindfulness isn't an aspirin you take at the end of your day to relieve your stress. Mindfulness is a seasoning that you use during your day to change the flavor!* —Peter M. Fellows

Practicing mindfulness is an ongoing process. It is not just a take-two-breaths-and-call-me-in-the-morning antidote to stress (although, like taking two aspirins and taking two breaths can certainly bring relief.) Cultivating a sense of mindfulness can give one a sense of calm and poise among the noise. Just as aspirin does not cure our headache or repair our muscle strain but only gives a sense of distance from the affliction facing us, mindfulness does not cure the stress and strains of life but offers a sense of distance from them. And just as getting to the gym regularly eventually strengthens our bodies, working out in the mindfulness gym helps

[2] *17 fatalities, 736 crashes: The shocking toll of Tesla's Autopilot Crashes have surged in the past four years, reflecting the hazards associated with increasingly widespread use of Tesla's futuristic driver-assistance tech.* The Washington Post, June 10, 2023, https://apple.news/AsoIfjsp6SwyCmWM8JPo9Bg.

strengthen our ability to face what life brings with greater equanimity, a different perspective that allows us to continue despite the buffeting, whirling winds around us. The formal and informal practices mentioned earlier and which we will further explore later, are meant to be ongoing. And yes, while it is true that taking a pause for a few mindful breaths during stressful moments can provide a sense of space and relief from the immediate stressor, the regular practice of pausing for mindful breaths, even when no stressors are present, builds our mindfulness muscle. In a sense, builds our ability to more readily handle whatever we are facing. It's almost as if we build up a reserve. Just as it is easier to run a 5k when one has been jogging every day, and it is easier to lift a fifty-pound bag of dog food when one has been lifting at the gym, exercising mindfulness even when we don't need it helps us when we do.

Mindfulness Is Not Complicated

> *When your attention moves into the Now, there is an alertness. It is as if you were waking up from a dream, the dream of thought, the dream of past and future. Such clarity, such simplicity. No room for problem-making. Just this moment as it is.* —Eckhart Tolle

Mindfulness is not complicated. In fact, little else is simpler. I mean, just tune in! Mindfulness means bringing your attention to the present moment. You can do it anywhere. You may do it sitting, you may do it standing, you may do it lying down. You may do it walking, you may do it talking, you may do it in town. You may do it at the beach, or in the mountains, or in the city near the fountains. You may do it hiking, you may do it biking. You may do it anyway and anywhere to your liking.

You need no special equipment. No need for a gym or fancy gear. No special footwear, no compression sleeves, no knee braces.

You. Just. Need. You. You may practice any-. Any-hour, any-day, any-where.

Really, want can be simpler? Midterms are done; you've reviewed them. Now forget them! Why continue to beat yourself up over them? Final exams are months away, do not fret about them; you have time to prepare. Instead, just tune in and pay attention to what is happening today. Right now. At this moment. Not past midterm exam moments. Not future final exam moments. The time to take midterms was back then when you took them. The time to take finals will be when you take them. Notice the use of the past tense "was" and future tense "will be"; neither of them is "now". Do not concern yourself with what was or what will be. Chances are that neither your midterms nor your finals are happening right now. (And if they are happening right now, maybe you should put this book down and go study? You can pick me back up when your exams are over; I'll still be here.)

You already lived last week last week. Leave it there. And the time to live next month will be next month. Mindfulness asks a simple question. What is happening right now? Right now, this moment, this instant? Not last week's, last month's, or last year's moments. Not next week's, next month's, or next year's moments. This instant moment right in front of you, this moment surrounding you. Let's check-in to "now".

Lift your eyes from the page for a few minutes and take in what is going on around you. What is happening right now? What can your senses tell you? Wherever you are, what can you see, feel, smell, taste, or hear? Stop. Listen. Look around. What do you see? What do you hear? What do you feel? Standing or sitting, can you feel your feet touching the ground? If you are sitting, can you feel your bottom in the seat? Are you inside or outdoors? Is it noisy? Quiet? How bright is the room or the outdoor space? If you are outside, is it bright, overcast, or dark? Are you warm, cold, or like the third bowl of porridge, just right? Set a timer for three minutes and just experience "now". What does now sound like? What do you hear? Does your nose detect any scents wafting through the air? A student once reported that he smelled delicious smells from a restaurant across the street from one of his favorite park benches. He told the class how he had been visiting that bench for many years, and that although the restaurant had always been there, he only just detected its aromas when he practiced mindfulness. In this moment, do you feel the sunlight or wind touch you? Any aromas wafting past? Just take three minutes to explore.

How did that go? You weren't focused on any exams, were you? And that's the point. The time you want to be 100 percent completely focused on an exam is when you are seated in the exam room taking the exam. Not now. (That being said, I hope you study throughout the semester and not wait to cram at the end.)

Of course, not thinking and worrying about exams doesn't mean you should ignore them; you should prepare for exams throughout the semester. Successful law students know they succeed by preparing for final exams day by day and that it is best to prepare throughout the semester. Preparing for tomorrow's class by reading and wrestling with the assigned cases tonight helps you prepare for tomorrow's class as well as for the inevitable final exams to come, but your focus tonight is on reading and learning the assigned cases; your focus is not on worries about the final exam itself. Studying is the only thing you should focus on during your scheduled study period. There will be time to focus on the final exam come final exam time. You know what it feels like to focus on exams; you've done it countless times. Think about it. I bet you can immerse yourself in that feeling right now by remembering any past exam. The heightened energy in your body as you get dressed and head towards campus. How you feel as you enter the exam room. As you take your seat. As you situate yourself. As you. . . .

Okay, now stop! You don't have to feel that exam tension anymore right now. Right now, you are reading about mindfulness. Right now, all you need to focus on are the words in front of you. Let go of the stress of upcoming final exams. There will be plenty of time to feel that stress when you take them—which will be during your scheduled exam moment at the end of the semester, not now. To help you focus on any matter at hand (reading for tomorrow's class, for example), eliminate or minimize distractions. Hint: leave the portals-to-everywhere-but-here in another room, in your purse, or in your car.

Note that the worry rule also applies to the ultimate, final-final exam, the bar exam held each February and July. You do not ignore the bar exam, you prepare for the bar exam incrementally day-by-day[3] by preparing for classes every day throughout law school, but there is no need to dwell on the bar exam while you are studying for classes. The time to address and focus on the bar exam will come. And at that time, you will see how pointless it was to fret and worry about what by then will seem like silly, inconsequential law school midterm and final exams. (You just cannot see that as easily from this side of the exams, although practicing mindfulness can help.)

Mindfulness Is Not a Destination

> *It's not the destination, it's the journey.* —Ralph Waldo Emerson

Mindfulness is not a destination. Although we can directly experience the present moment, now, by immersing ourselves in it in a mindful manner, we never arrive at a place called mindfulness. We practice mindfulness just as doctors practice medicine, just as lawyers practice law. Learning about the human body and various

---

[3] See Dennis J. Tonsing, *1000 Days to the Bar But the Practice of Law Begins Now* 3d ed. (William S. Hein & Co., Inc. 2022).

medical procedures is only the beginning of a lifelong journey of practicing medicine. Doctors never arrive at a place called medicine. Likewise, learning the body of law and various courtroom procedures is only the beginning of a lifelong journey of practicing law. Lawyers never arrive at a place called law. Learning about our ever-shifting body of thoughts and various mindful procedures to bring ourselves to the present moment is only the beginning of a lifelong journey of practicing mindfulness. We never arrive at a place called mindfulness. Every doctor forges her own way forward, along her own practice towards medicine. Every lawyer forges his own way forward, along his own practice towards law. And everyone pursuing mindfulness forges their own way forward, along his or her own practice towards it.

Experienced practitioners of mindfulness techniques continue to practice for the same reasons we continue to work out and exercise. We do not suddenly arrive at a place called fitness or achieve fitness and then walk away from it. Through trial and error, or perhaps with the help of a fitness coach, we learn that we can improve our fitness incrementally, and we may even reach a point where we feel "fit enough", but we don't stop exercising. We learned that we only remain fit by continually practicing healthy lifestyle choices concerning food, sleep, exercise, hydration, and stress management. Practicing mindfulness techniques certainly helps us manage stress better, and so much more. Learning to eat mindfully can help improve your diet—"I ate fewer cookies," "I only needed three wings instead of my usual six"—exercising mindfully can help improve your workout, and, having fallen asleep myself while meditating; I know practicing meditation improves sleep! Practicing mindfulness may not improve your hydration, but who knows? Remember what one student said: "Even the water I drank tasted crisper." I promise that if you drink a glass of water mindfully, it will be a more pleasant experience than gulping one down.

What Mindfulness Is

Mindfulness isn't just a cool app; Mindfulness is an incredibly powerful operating system! —Peter M. Fellows

There are five major components to Mindfulness:

- Paying attention to what is presently unfolding
- Open awareness of what is presently unfolding
- Acceptance of what is presently unfolding
- Not identifying with what is presently unfolding
- Understanding you always have a choice on how to respond

Let's look at them one at a time.

Paying Attention to What Is Presently Unfolding

Paying attention to what is presently unfolding simply means staying in the moment, staying in the room, and staying with the matter at hand or the people you are with while avoiding distractions, including our ubiquitous portals-to-anywhere-but-here.

Open Awareness of What Is Presently Unfolding

Now that we are paying attention to the moment unfolding, really become aware of the moment. Slow down instead of defaulting to our usual mode of hurriedly skimming over the present in a hurry to get to what is next. What is next is another moment. Soak the moments in; really experience them. Use all five senses.

Acceptance of What Is Presently Unfolding

The next stage is to resist judging, naming, or labeling what is unfolding; just experience it instead. This is easier said than done because we are taught since we are young to discriminate and judge what we encounter. When we listen to music, unless we are music critics, our job is not to decide if the music is good or bad, our job is to just listen. (Note, this doesn't mean you have to keep listening to music you don't enjoy.)

Not Identifying with What Is Presently Unfolding

Accepting what is unfolding and not identifying with what is unfolding are two different things. Take a toothache, for example. Accepting that I have a toothache, that it hurts, that I don't like it, and that I can't wait until a dentist fixes it, is one thing. Identifying with the toothache causes me to believe that I am the toothache when in fact I am so much more. The immediacy of the pain makes it too easy to identify with the toothache, in fact it is hard to think about anything else. Same thing after stubbing a toe. The shooting pain, seeing red, and loud exclamations that follow are automatic; we don't feel like much more than a stubbed toe. But we are more than our toe, more than our tooth. We are more than our pain and more than our thoughts. We are more than what currently has captured our attention.

Understanding You Always Have a Choice on How to Respond to What is Presently Unfolding

> *The ancestor of every action is a thought.* —Ralph Waldo Emerson

> *Between stimulus and response, there is a space. In that space is our power to choose our response. In our response lies our growth and our freedom.* —Victor Frankl

You always have a choice to decide how you will relate to what is presently unfolding. We need to understand that no matter what is unfolding, we have a choice in how we respond. We may only make this choice, however, after we have made room for decision-making instead of succumbing to well-worn, knee-jerk reactions. We need not remain stoic and accept what is as is; always having a choice means we can choose how to react (or if we react at all). The room is cold? We may choose to stay and shiver because the meeting will be over in just a few minutes; we may choose to put on a sweater or jacket; we may choose to step outside the room or into the sunshine, or we may ask someone to address the room temperature. We always have a choice. Too often, however, we do not exercise our prerogative to choose. Practicing mindfulness helps us to make room for choices.

Among other things, mindfulness is a way to seemingly slow things down. Maybe I'm old-fashioned, but I still enjoy crossing campus today as I did 200 years ago when I was a law student, that is, without the internet glued to my fingers. I figure that life moves at me fast enough and that I want to at least enjoy my walk across campus. I want to see, feel, and experience the blue skies and palm trees, not just a text or bit of newsfeed scrolling on my portal-to-everywhere-but-here. I am not the first to want to slow things down a bit; humans have longed to slow things down for thousands of years. Here are a few examples.

Buddha, Christ, Thoreau, and the Hippies

> *The fact that human beings do not just passively receive life events, but instead we selectively perceive, constantly interpret, automatically judge, and sometimes unwittingly create our own reality has been central to traditions that, for centuries, have emphasized mindfulness and centering practices.* —Dr. Lisa Finlay.[4]

4 *How You Think About Stress Matters* https://www.headington-institute.org/blog/resource/how-you-think-about-stress-matters/.

> *Be where you are; otherwise you will miss your life.* —Buddha

> *Do not worry about tomorrow, for tomorrow will worry about itself. Each day has enough trouble of its own.* —Christ

> *Don't destroy your peace of mind by looking back, worrying about the past. Live in the present.* —David Thoreau

> *Turn on, tune in, drop out.* —Timothy Leary

The foundation of mindfulness is Buddhism. Buddha first emphasized mindfulness as a key to spiritual development over 2,500 years ago. He found it essential to develop wisdom and attain inner peace. Five hundred years, later around 2,000 years ago, Christ taught his followers his version of tomorrow taking care of itself.[5] The words vary in the different translations of the Bible, but the message remains the same. Henry David Thoreau sat at Walden's Pond in the 1800s and told us. And, of course, in the 1960s, hippies were turning on, tuning in, and dropping out without the mind-altering capabilities of the internet; other mind-altering avenues prevailed.

I remember a conversation with my Aunt Peggy when I was either a young teen or maybe a tween. It was during a family reunion, big affairs with my large, extended family. I don't remember how the conversation came up, probably because I overheard an adult remark something about, "Well, it's the start of another summer. Where does the time go?" I told my aunt that I, too, noticed how time had sped up. "The time between Thanksgiving and Christmas was almost unbearable when I was little," I said. "And summers used to be boring and lasted way too

---

5 Mathew 6:34.

long." (I was weird; I liked school.) Summers and the wait for Christmas, I told her, weren't so long now.

"Oh, son," she told me. "I'm so sorry you sense that already because I've got bad news for you; once you learn that, time only continues speeding up. You will see! Enjoy today because many tomorrows will have passed when you blink and next look up." Something in her demeanor that day made me understand that she was sharing wisdom. And of course, she was right. You know it too; you have already experienced your own life speeding up. I recently quipped to a colleague that we don't even get to enjoy an entire summer anymore; it seems to me that what was once a hot, boring, and terribly long summer is now just a hot, terribly short three-day holiday weekend. I call it the Memorial-Fourth-of-Labor-Day-Weekend. When Memorial Day comes around, you can practically reach out and touch July Fourth, and by July Fourth back-to-school-sales have begun and Labor Day seems two breaths away.

Experiencing Fully the Present Moment

What is essential is lived in the present. —Martin Buber

To fully experience the present moment, we must be absorbed in, focused on, and open to what is unfolding now. Two examples of activities that keep me in the moment are working jigsaw puzzles and reading good works. I can't put either a good puzzle or a good book away. Both activities have carried me late into the night without regard for mornings. I enjoy reading and puzzling in large part because they allow me great escape—an off switch—from my mind. Escape from incessant, perpetual, and unrelenting thoughts that dance, wave, and wriggle for my attention. When working a puzzle, I can only fixate on the shapes and colors of the pieces lying around, rotating pieces in my hand and in my mind's eye to match them with their permanent home. There is no room for other thoughts. "Will this fit here?" consumes me. Likewise, when I get hold of a page-turner of a book—Property Law anyone?—hours often fly by until I discover, yipes, I should have turned the light out three hours ago! When reading like that, I am fully concentrated on bringing the story alive to my mind's eyes and ears, building the scene as I imagine it to be. The author, the words, my room disappears. My mind isn't turned off; rather it is turned on, energized, excited, and focused.

While reading or working a puzzle I do not have to shoosh my mind. I do not have to turn it off. I do not have to tell it to behave; I just focus on what is ahead of me. Simple opportunities to fully experience any present moment abound; if you think about it, every single moment has opportunities. Any activity will do. We can choose to focus on any activity we engage in. From walking the dog, washing the dishes, taking the trash out, and everything in between.

The Five Senses

Some feel the quickest way into any moment, the quickest great escape from the incessant, relentless thoughts and doing that unconsciously fill our lives is through the five senses.

Sight

Wherever you are, look around. Once I taught my mindfulness class in a classroom with a locked closet. A student on her way to use the restroom found it necessary to first check the closet door to see what was behind it or if it was locked. (It was locked as always.) I thought her detour curious but paid little attention to it otherwise. Later in class, during a break between exercises, the student suddenly blurted out, "Professor Ahlers, what's behind that door, and where does it go!?"

"It is a closet," I replied. "And it is locked; it doesn't lead anywhere." I was fascinated when one after another, three students who had each already taken separate classes in the room shared that they had no idea the closet was there until their classmate that day tried the door. They had never seen the prominent wooden door embedded in the otherwise pale-yellow wall. (It's not a little door.) When they asked when and why the school put the closet there, all I could say was that it predated me and that it had been there for more than twenty years.

My students' experience is not uncommon. Most of us, most of the time, don't see what is in front of us—okay, the door was off to the side, but it wasn't a large room, and it was a large door—instead, we bury ourselves in yesterdays, tomorrows, and somewhere elses. I mentioned earlier how remarkable I find students navigating campus, deftly avoiding obstacles without ever looking up from their precious portals to anywhere but here. Some sort of Apple, Google, or Tesla radar, I guess.

Put your portal down and look around wherever you are. It doesn't matter if you are enjoying the vistas of the Grand Canyon or the interior doldrums of a law school classroom; you can train yourself to look and see what is in front of you and never have to have a closet door sneak up on you again!

If you are outside, is it day, night, dusk, or dawn? What color is the sky? Is it sunny, cloudy, or just partly cloudy? (What does partly cloudy mean in a weather report anyway; when does partly cloudy become cloudy? Or sunny, for that matter?) If there are clouds, how fast are they moving? Are they leisurely floating by or really booking it across the sky? Are they invitingly white and fluffy or menacingly dark and brooding? Are there any trees? Grass? Birds? Squirrels? Maybe the moon is out, stars and planets too. Can you name any stars or planets? There are a lot of stars, aren't there?

Maybe you are indoors, standing in front of an elevator. What color is the elevator door? What shape and color are the elevator buttons? Are others waiting for the elevator too? If so, what colors are they wearing? What color is the floor? Carpet? Tiles? What colors are the walls? What do the light fixtures look like? Where is the closest fire alarm? Look around and notice—really see things. See the awe surrounding us.

Dr. Dacher Keltner, a psychology professor and author of *Awe: The New Science of Everyday Wonder and How It Can Transform Your Life*, explained that awe is a "complex emotion we experience when encountering something so vast that our sense of self recedes."[6] Dr. Keltner talks about how it is easy for most of us to feel our sense of self receding in the vast magnitude of awe and wonder felt when gazing at the Grand Canyon. He goes on to say how transformative developing the ability to see the awe surrounding us in the everyday ordinary can be. And, in a way, that is what mindfulness helps us do—appreciate the awe, the fullness, the richness of all that is unfolding right now. As we focus on what is in front of us, we cannot spend time worrying about yesterdays or tomorrows.

Hearing

Wherever you are, listen around you. What do you hear? If you are outside, are you in the city? At the beach? In the forest? I bet if you think about those locations, you can hear the sounds you would hear if you were there. Try it. Imagine the city. Do you hear the traffic? Are horns honking? Do you hear footsteps as pedestrians pass by? Imagine the beach. Do you hear the waves, the gulls, and the wind? Imagine walking along a path in a forest. Do you hear the wind in the trees? Birds? Perhaps squirrels scampering by?

If you are indoors, where? Are you in a mall? In a library? In a classroom? I bet if you think about those locations, you can hear the sounds you would hear if you were there. Try it. Imagine the mall. Do you hear parents cautioning children? Do you hear children

---

[6] Jancee Dunn, New York Times, *This Kind of Walk Is Much More Than a Workout: Incorporating awe into your daily stroll can bring mental and physical benefits. Here's how to get started.* (New York Times Well, June 2, 2023).

enjoying themselves? Can you hear the hum of the food court, everyone deciding what to eat? Imagine a library. Can you hear the quiet? Do you hear hushed conversations? Perhaps you hear the occasional door opening and closing. Maybe you are standing in front of an elevator. Can you hear the elevator motor after you press the call button? Do you hear pinging sounds wafting down the elevator shaft as your chariot approaches? Are others waiting for the elevator? If so, are they quiet or chatty?

How readily we can bring these inside and outside places alive in our minds, yet most often fail to bring alive the very scene currently unfolding and directly surrounding us. It is easy to become mindful of any present moment—just ask yourself, what do I hear?

And don't listen just to identify the sound: that's a cough, a car, a siren a plane. Listen to and focus on the aural sensation. Is the sound high-pitched? Low? Is the sound near or coming from afar? Loud? Soft? Pleasant or un? Listen to and experience the sound. The idea is not to identify the sound, not to name it, but just to listen to it. To just hear it.

Touch

Wherever you are and whatever you are doing, ask yourself what you can perceive through your sense of touch. If you are sitting, can you make yourself aware of the feeling of your feet touching the floor? Can you feel your bottom in the chair or sofa? Is your back against the backrest? Can you feel this book in your hand? When it is time, ask yourself what it feels like to turn a page. Do you use your thumb or forefinger to turn it? Which hand holds the book as the other turns the page? Is the temperature comfortable? No matter if you are wearing shorts or are bundled up; perhaps you are in your pajamas. Can you feel your clothing touch your skin?

Maybe you are indoors, standing in front of an elevator. Can you make yourself aware of your legs balancing your weight and your feet touching the floor? Are you carrying books or a knapsack? Can you feel their weight in your hands or on your shoulders? And the elevator call button, what does it feel like? Is it rough or smooth? Which finger do you use to press it? What does it feel like to press the button? How hard did you press it? Did you press it more than once?

If you are lying down, can you feel where your heels, legs, hips, bottom, back, shoulders, and head touch the mattress? Are you on top of the blankets or snuggled underneath them? What does that feel like?

And if you are working out, playing a sport, cleaning the house, washing dishes, folding laundry, or grocery shopping, you can always drop in and ask yourself what your body senses right then. Notice your heart rate. Are you out of breath? Washing dishes? Feel the soapy dishwater; is it hot, cold, warm? Folding clothes? Notice the texture and weight of your bath towels versus the texture and weight of your underwear. Grocery shopping? Actively notice and feel the weight, size, shape, and textures you encounter as you select your fruits and vegetables. Of course, you might as well incorporate the sense of sight and look at their various colors, sizes, shapes, and textures too. You might smell them as well, but I'd hold off on tasting them until they are paid for.

Smell

Wherever you are, what does it smell like? There are scents in the air. Sometimes scents seem more readily available than others, like when we are in the kitchen preparing a meal or at a restaurant preparing to enjoy one—but scents abound everywhere. If you are outside, do you smell fresh air? Salt air? Car fumes? Has it just rained? Any flowers blooming? Anyone passing by wearing perfume or cologne? Are you wearing perfume or cologne? Scents are everywhere. At the beach, in the forest, on the street, in your car, in your classroom and grocery store, in Starbucks, and in Target too. In the shower, your soap and shampoo provide their own biome. Perhaps that was what the artist formerly known as the artist formerly known as Prince meant with his lyric, "I, I, I smell myself".[7]

Taste

Wherever you are, stop and taste it. Taste is closely tied to our sense of smell. For example, if you imagine a favorite indulgence, let's say your favorite pizza, chances are if you recall its ooey gooey steaming fresh from the oven smell, you will taste it as well. (Be careful not to burn the roof of your mouth.) Most of us think of taste only while eating or drinking—new bottle of wine, anyone?—but anyone who has spent any time around infants can attest to the fact that they taste. . . everything! It is part of their exploration process as they try to make sense of the world around them. While I do not recommend tasting everything in the world around us, practicing mindfulness does help us rediscover the "beginner's mind", or the ability to look at the world as we once did, in awe and exploration instead of just cruising through our days on autopilot. Jon Kabat-Zinn discusses the beginner's mind using an encounter with a dog—no, we don't taste the dog. Here's Jon:

> Have you ever looked at a dog and really seen it in its total "dogness"? A dog is quite miraculous when you really see it. What is it? Where did it come from? Where is it going? What is it doing here? Why is it shaped the way it is? What is its "view" of things, of the neighborhood? What are its feelings?
>
> Children tend to think about things this way. Their vision is fresh. They see things as if for the first time every time. Sometimes our seeing gets tired. We just see a dog: "If you've seen one dog, you've seen them all." So we

---

7 Prince. *Prettyman*, RaveUn2 The Joy Fantastic (1999).

barely see it at all. We tend to see more through our thoughts and opinions than through our eyes. Our thoughts act as a kind of veil, preventing us from seeing things with fresh eyes. What comes into view is identified by the thinking, categorizing mind and quickly framed: a dog. This frame of mind actually prevents us from seeing the dog in its fullness. It processes and categorizes the "dog" signal and all its various associations very quickly in our brain and then moves on to do the same with the next perception or thought.[8]

Movie Theater of the Mind

Thoughts are things. —Prentice Mulford

Our thoughts act as a kind of veil, preventing us from seeing things with fresh eyes. —Jon Kabat-Zinn

Observe your thoughts, don't believe them. —Eckhart Tolle

Who doesn't like a good night at the movies? If not out in a cool, dark theater, then perhaps curled up at home with a favorite person or people and Netflix? (Unless you got booted off the family account.) No matter where or how we access our movies, we watch movies for entertainment. To relax, to escape, to unwind, to enjoy ourselves. . .to temporarily step aside from our responsibilities. That's all fine, wonderful, and good. We know, however, no matter how mesmerizing or absorbing the movie is, that the movie is not reality. Even period pieces which burst alive with expert costuming, authentic contemporary dialog, and excellent acting that suck us in, swoop us away and receive twelveteen Oscar nominations are not real. At the end of the movie, as the credits begin to roll, and the

[8] Jon Kabat-Zinn. *Full Catastrophe Living* 175 Revised and updated ed. (Bantam Books (2013)).

lights go up just a little—so the people who don't want to read fifteen minutes of tiny scrolling text crediting each and every second- and third-assistant sandwich delivery person who participated—we know we are about to return to the real world. We stretch and lift our eyes from the screen and begin to run our eyes around the theater instead. Eventually we stand, grab our empty giant soda cup and our near-empty giant bucket of popcorn—more on the popcorn later—and head for the aisles.

No matter how well-acclaimed the film, no matter how far in it sucked us, and no matter how far away it took us, deep down somewhere we knew we weren't watching real life unfold. And even if the movie so wowed us that we forgot we were sitting in a theater, eventually the credits begin to roll and the lights come up, and we are nudged gently back to reality.

Why do I bring all this up? I bring all this up because I find the movie analogy useful in discussing how sometimes, ofttimes, what is only flickering images appearing to be in motion before us is interpreted to be real life. In the movie theater, we intentionally select a particular set of flickering images to watch, images produced by artists and craftsmen for our pleasure. In the theater of our minds, we are subject to flickering images (thoughts) to watch, thoughts and images produced by us, but for what purpose? And, unfortunately, in the theater of our mind, no one is turning the house lights up and reminding us to go home. We have to do it.

Let's go back into the movie theater first. You find your seat, the lights come down, and the previews start. There is the part of you that watches the movie, the corporal part of you that experiences the movie through your senses, primarily your eyes and ears—but can't you taste that ice-cold Coca-Cola when you hear those bubbles in the ads?—and the part of you which watches you watch the movie, the part of you that interprets what the senses perceive. The part of you that hides your eyes and covers your ears during the scary parts while another member of the audience gives off a nervous laugh, and another one chuckles. Different people can interpret the same moving pictures in different ways. It makes sense that different people with different perspectives can see and interpret things differently. In fact, mindfulness will teach you that even you can learn to approach, see, and interpret the same scene in the same movie of life in different ways. I've believed since I was young that even the same person sitting in a different seat in the same theater could change their perspective, interpretation, and experience of the movie because of the different viewpoints the different seats offered. Ever sit way, way, way up front, almost under the screen?

I don't remember why, but I started playing a game as a boy where, never physically leaving my seat in the theater, I would imagine myself watching the movie from other seats. Watching from up closer on the left-hand side of the theater. Now from further back on the right. Now dead center in the back row where all the teenagers were making out. Years later, I realized I was keeping myself aware of that part of me who was watching me watch the movie. Still with me? It may have been James Bond or John Wayne. There was a story being told, the flickering pictures, and then there was me interpreting the story and flickering pictures.

Sticking with the analogy of the movie theater, the "images" in the theater of the mind are our thoughts, not still pictures presented as if in motion. Our thoughts present themselves as if they are real, just as real actors play their characters as if they are real. And, of course, in one sense, both the characters in the film and the thoughts in our minds are real; an author created the characters, and we created our thoughts. The characters are an amalgamation of fiction at best. And so are our thoughts. However, while there is little danger of mistaking the current Marvel action film as an accurate portrait of society today, there is a significant danger of accepting the thoughts streaming across the screen of our consciousness as truth just because we saw it or thought it. The more we encourage and involve the part of us which watches us watch our thoughts, the better chance we have for discerning the whole truths. Thoughts are things, but not all thoughts are true. *Our thoughts act as a kind of veil, preventing us from seeing things with fresh eyes.*[9]

The difference between movie theaters and theaters of the mind is that we go to movie theaters to temporarily escape reality, while we seldom escape the nonreality of the thoughts playing in the theaters of our mind. We consciously choose to escape to the one and would benefit from consciously choosing to escape now and again from the latter. Our minds are extraordinary, and our capacity to think is a powerful tool. There are times for thinking, countless appropriate times for thinking, just not constantly.

Thoughts are things, and thoughts are powerful. Thoughts help us plan and achieve. You are a law student. You weren't always a law student. At some point, the thought of going to law school "occurred" to you, arose within you. How did the thought of you attending law school first arise? It may have been suggested to you, or you may have come up with it by yourself. You may have read about it, heard about it, or met a lawyer. It doesn't matter. The thought of you attending law school and becoming a lawyer arose within you, a thought bubble in the theater of your mind. But it takes more than one thought to make things happen. More thought bubbles and many more questions have to be asked and answered. You might have asked yourself, for example, how do I even get to law school? Where are law schools located? How much do law schools cost? How long does law school take? Whom can I talk to about all these questions about going to law school?

---

[9] Jon Kabat-Zinn. *Full Catastrophe Living* 175 Revised and updated ed. (Bantam Books (2013)).

To get here, into law school, you had to think, plan, and make decisions, all requiring thinking, excellent uses for thinking! Everything around you, except for what naturally occurs in nature, everything else you can see, feel, taste, touch, and smell, existed first in someone's mind before existing in our physical world. Someone had to think it, imagine it in their mind, before they could create it and bring it into the physical world. Little things like this book or a paper clip and big things like Interstate highways or the Empire State Building. Simple things like scrap paper and complex things like the James Webb Space Telescope. We put a man on the moon as the result of many years of meticulous thinking and planning.

So yes, thoughts are things, thoughts are powerful, and thoughts are important. But what lies behind the thoughts (some say between them) is more important; is paramount. Too often, however, we get lost in the incessant chatter of our thoughts instead. It is akin to focusing on the few clouds in the sky and forgetting about the infinite blue surrounding them. We get caught up in doing, doing, doing instead of just being. Caught up in cloud jumping instead of just cloud watching. Mindfulness helps us learn to watch, to experience being. Being is the part of you sitting in the movie theater watching you watch the movie and the part of you in the theater in your mind that watches you watch your thoughts. Just as there is more to your life than the movie that just ended, there is more to your life than the thoughts that stream incessantly across your mind's theater screen. Like seeing a dog in all its dogness instead of seeing its shorthand thought: dog. When we take the time to experience the dog in all its dogness, it tends to make time seem to slow down; we are not as caught up in mere rapid-fire shorthand thoughts.

Mindfulness is not about slowing or stopping thoughts—we simply can't turn off our thought bubble generators. We can, however, change our focus and look away from the screen in our mind from time to time. These pauses make the space between our thoughts seem to grow, which in turn seems to make our thoughts slow down. We see more dogs in all their dogness and fewer shorthand thoughts: dog. Life is short enough as it is, yet most of the time, we cruise through life on autopilot, cheating ourselves out of the full experience of dogness, settling for truncated thoughts: dog.

Mindfulness v. Mindlessness

> *Mindfulness makes a year feel like a decade, whereas mindlessness does the opposite.* —Mokokoma Mokhonoana
>
> *Mindlessness often leads to headlessness.* —Mokokoma Mokhonoana

Eckhart Tolle, whose 1997 book *The Power of Now* was instrumental in getting me more curious about mindfulness, does not like using the word mindfulness because he feels it suggests a fully active mind while the full power and majesty of any given moment is best experienced without thought rather than with thought. You may get a sense of what Tolle is talking about if you have ever watched the sun setting into the sea, *sinking like a ship.*[10]

For me, it is mesmerizing how the sun almost imperceptibly yields to gravity, how its colors and the surrounding sky change from yellow to orange to red to twilight to gone. Sometimes I swear I can heal a sizzle when it finally touches the water. I hear my father's voice as he stood behind me years ago on a beach. I brought my camera to try to catch the sunset. "Look," he said, his hands on my shoulders. "Just look, son. Soak it in. You can't capture all of this in your camera, but you can capture it here," he told me as he

[10] Bob Dylan, *Meet Me in the Morning* from *Blood on the Tracks* (Columbia Records, (1975)).

placed the palm of his hand over my heart. "Sometimes," he told me, "I think I can hear a sizzle when it finally touches the water. Let's listen."

Of course, many photographers have created many magnificent photographs of setting suns; my father wasn't, and Eckhart isn't saying that you cannot adequately photograph the setting sun, their point is that there is so much more going on while the sun is setting than what can be seen through the camera's lens. While a skilled photographer can indeed capture a stunning sunset and a gifted photographer might even capture a bit of wonder, still, the photograph is filtered, framed, and limited by the skills of the photographer. A photographer resting his camera will experience a different sunset because instead of focusing through one lens, all his senses are open and alive and experiencing the sinking ship. If he placed his camera down, that same photographer would experience a different sunset because instead of focusing all his senses through one lens, he would be open, expanded, and fully experiencing the sinking sun; he might even hear it touch the water, tsssss.

Actively watching the sunset instead of trying to capture a slice of it on camera captures an essence of mindfulness: paying attention to what is unfolding instead of letting life fly by and pretending to be present for it thinking, *I got a picture of it so I can always remember*. I don't have a picture of the sunset I saw with my dad that evening, but I sure can see it. I feel the sand on my feet, the wind in my hair, his hands on my shoulder. I smell and taste the salty air, and I hear the gulls, the wind, and yes, even the sizzle as the sun touches the water. In that moment my father taught me to pay attention to what was happening in the moment instead of rushing past the moment my life on automatic pilot.

Automatic Pilot

The benefits of engaging autopilot are countless. Mundane, tedious tasks requiring minimal attention can run in the background and free us up for more interesting tasks. For example, faced with navigating a passenger jet in pitch darkness 35,000 feet over an ocean for six hours, why not let the computer do it?—well, any computer other than HAL, of course. But as so often happens in life, it is possible to have too much of a good thing. We all overuse autopilot. In fact, some days it seems we rarely consciously pilot. From the moment we awaken, as we go, go, go, all day, right until the moment we stumble back to sleep, precious little time is spent focused on our lives unfolding before us. And most often, when rare unscheduled moments slip past the guards to our scheduled lives, opportunities for pause and rest from the torrid pace of our days, we squander the moments with cute YouTube or TikTok cat videos or some other distraction.

Autopilot Morning

Think about it. When I ask my students what they do first when they wake up, almost everyone says they reach for their phones. Almost always a one hundred percent response rate. Every time. Not take a moment to think *good morning, me, good morning, day, or good morning, honey*; *just where's my phone*? Is that you first thing in the morning?

Who knows? Someone may have texted me or, worse, posted a cute cat video that I may have missed! Can't get out of bed without checking! Maybe Professor Ahlers canceled Property class; that'd be nice! Twenty minutes later, you suddenly realize how far away the portal-to-anywhere-but-here took you, and you jump up, exclaiming, "Goodness"! (Or something more earthy) "I'm going to be late! You jump in the shower, almost dry your hair, toss on some clothes, maybe shave, or apply makeup, grab a couple of bites of something for breakfast, swig a little coffee, grab your keys, head out the door, and drive to campus. If you are lucky, maybe you remember to peck someone's cheek goodbye.

We take showers but are rarely ever really in the shower. We dry ourselves off but rarely feel the towel. We get dressed while rehearsing our day and find our keys. We may or may not have had time for a bite of something to eat, but don't ask us what it was because we can't remember. If we are just a little late but not a lotta late, we stop for a latte. Swing by Starbucks to slurp one down before class.

That's an autopilot morning. How about a non-autopilot morning? What might one of those look like? I asked my students.

Non-Autopilot Morning

After we wake up, many of us shower. Read what three students told me about their fully piloted showers.

Piloted Shower 1:

> Today my mindful activity was taking a shower. I was in a rush to go somewhere, so I timed it to ten minutes. I set my alarm on my phone and went in, fully focused on my shower only. Normally, I'll play some music and let the shower go on autopilot mode, but this time I didn't do that. I allowed myself to focus on hearing the sound of the water droplets hitting my shower floor. I heard the sound of the lathering when I applied my body wash to my whole body and the conditioner to my hair. I visually became aware of the steam created because my water temperature was scolding hot. I focused on the feeling of that hot water and the way it felt running against my skin. I also really enjoyed the silence I felt. There was a sense of peace for me, even if it only lasted for a ten-minute

period. I realized I was very much more self-aware of my body than I usually am in my showers. This shower became a very peaceful, relaxing, and positive experience for me. I really did notice things that I usually pay no mind to, like the little bubbles that are created when I'm about to apply soap. Their size, their shapes, even their colors. Some of them looked almost rainbow-like. I really noticed the texture of my fingertips as they started to get wet. I even noticed how there was this refreshing feeling when I got out and was done with the shower.

Piloted Shower 2:

The shower water fills the air with warm steam.

The temperature shifts significantly from before the shower was turned on.

Condensation forms on the mirror and little droplets on the counter.

The water feels hot on my skin but comfortable as I'm still. The shower water fills

The soap smells like roses.

I can almost hear each bubble of the lather popping

I can see the steam filling the air

I can hear the water dripping off the caddy

I feel more refreshed and relaxed.

Piloted Shower 3:

I put music on in the background to notice when I would get distracted because sometimes, I'm not aware until I hear myself singing along.

When I got into the shower, I felt the cold water hit my body. It felt nice as I had just finished working out. I

> felt how harsh the water was on my skin. Once I started to wash myself, I could feel the exfoliating glove and the how it was abrasive. I could smell the soap and body wash that I was using.
>
> It was a stress-relief body wash with eucalyptus and lavender. It made the water cooler on my skin, and it felt fresh. As I finished my shower it made me rethink how I experience my everyday mundane activities.

How did your last shower compare to these? No matter how you showered, you didn't shower wrong; you got yourself clean. You just probably cleaned up while preoccupied with something else, like preparing your to-do list for the day or reminding yourself to call your mom or the vet. One of the dividends of living mindfully, of paying attention to what is happening at the moment, of paying attention to taking a shower while in the shower, is that we begin to appreciate the value of life as it unfolds around us. The more we appreciate the shower just for being a shower, the more we can appreciate the rightful place for creating to-do lists and calls to Mom—just not in the shower.

After we've showered, many of us like a cup of coffee (while some of us need the caffeine fix before we can even face the shower). Here's what a student had to say about enjoying a coffee made at home with a Keurig.

> For the first time ever, I took the time to be mindful of my cup of coffee.
>
> I started by analyzing the K-cup: Eight O'Clock Coffee. The plastic container, its smoothness, and its colors (red, white, brown). Thereafter, I analyzed the packs of equal I use; reading the label of the light blue packet I noticed that while it's distributed by Mersiant US,

Inc. out of Chicago, it's made in Mexico. Never stopped to notice that—wow!

Next, my liquid Coffee Mate creamer; I felt the texture of the bottle and read the information on the label. But what drew most of my attention were the tiny letters at the bottom of the container's edge—"All trademarks are owned by Société Des Products Nestle S.A., Vevey, Switzerland or used with permission"—wow! Not made the U.S., either.

I proceeded to fill the Keurig machine with 1 cup (actually 6 ounces) of water, placed the K-cup in, and pressed "brew." I poured the creamer into my red ceramic Barry University mug, added 4 packets of equal, and patiently waited.

I noticed my breath (caught some of my wandering thoughts), and before I knew it the machine was making my coffee. Ah, the dripping noise, the pleasant aroma! As I stirred to mix the ingredients, I smelled the delicious coffee in the steamy mug.

At last, I sat in a quiet space, on my chair in the living room, and held the warm mug, as I contemplated the quiet stillness of my moment—no phones, no tv, no radio—just me and my coffee.

First time I'd ever peacefully enjoyed my coffee, with a clear, nonjudgmental, no rush, no worries on my mind, a fresh cup of coffee.

Definitely won't be my last.

Another student enjoyed his coffee with Spider-Man.

For today's mindful activity, I decided to drink coffee in the morning in my favorite Spider-Man mug.

> I stood on my porch and noticed how cold it was. Cold usually bothers me, but this time I let it pass and just enjoyed the weather. I sipped my coffee and took loud slurps, too, for fun (since I was alone) just to humor myself.
>
> I noticed how peaceful my community is in the morning, and I relaxed looking at people walking their pets and getting ready for their commute to work or wherever they had to be.
>
> I enjoyed the warmth the coffee gave me, especially with how cold it was. I drifted off into thoughts about how I could decorate my porch, where to put furniture, and so on, but I came back and tried to enjoy the moment longer.

I drank slowly, and I really enjoyed drinking coffee this time without being on automatic. I had a no phone, no school, no nothing policy. Just me and my Spider-Man mug drinking on a porch and being in the moment. Tried to enjoy every sensation that came with it. Time spent escaping autopilot and actively piloting our lives serves several functions. It tends to allow us more room to bring into focus what is happening and to appreciate each moment as it unfolds; a shower becomes more than just a way to come clean, a cup of coffee is more than a shot of caffeine. The more we appreciate and acknowledge what is going on at any moment we realize that there is a time and a place for everything, but just not now. Enjoying your shower is not going to make your final exams go away. Even a Superman coffee mug won't defeat mid-term and final exam stress, but during this shower, or this cup of coffee, or this lunch with my friends, this is not the time to make a to-do list or to stress about exams.

Another advantage to piloting our lives is that it helps us keep things in perspective. Even as crunch time nears, as classes wind down and the concomitant stress of exams starts rising, the longer and more often we can keep ourselves in the pilot's seat actively piloting and aware, the greater chance of experiencing a sense of having more space and gaining a different perspective, that finals are important—but that they aren't everything. You don't have to walk around muttering to yourself, *I'm gonna fail, I'm gonna fail, I'm gonna fail. I'm doomed.*

Preparing to pass your exams is important. And you have learned all semester long by being mindful, that it's also important to take care of yourself and your loved ones. You also have to bathe or shower, brush your teeth, exercise, eat, sleep, buy groceries, cook, get the dog to the vet, visit Mom, *etc.* I am not trying to equate two minutes of wrestling with a toothbrush brushing your teeth with three- and four-hour final exams where students might wrestle with *International Shoe*'s minimum contacts or *Palsgraf's* foreseeable harm, however, the more moments we experience everything we do helps us appreciate everything we do and helps us put everything we do in perspective. *Yes, it's exam time. I'm stressed. That's okay, it's exam time. It's okay to be stressed. No need to overdo the stress. We got this. Right now, it's time to take a shower, listen to some music, and get some sleep.*

Reasons for Not Autopiloting

Reasons for not autopiloting include gaining a greater sense of space and time around us, of expanding a sense of distance between when stimuli reach us and when we react to the stimuli. A sense that there is more breathing room between what is occurring and what our response to a situation may be. When we are stressed and when we are unconsciously autopiloting, we tend to react to our surroundings automatically without thinking and rarely take time to consider alternate responses. Regularly practicing mindfulness seems to open things up, slow time down, and generally allow a sense of freedom we miss when we barrel unconsciously through life. This greater sense of space grows out of a greater appreciation for our complete surroundings. The more we pay attention to all that is immediately unfolding around us, the greater sense of peace we gain from seeing and feeling ourselves and belonging to a greater world, a wider, bigger, and more fantastic and interesting experience than the tiny narrow screen world our portals-to-anywhere-but-here launched us. While we stay present, we have an opportunity to choose among alternative responses instead of being dragged off—we don't even know why—perhaps to some newsfeed blog somewhere or to yet another cute cat video.

This expanding space is not derived from a sense of boxing up thoughts, ideas, problems, and troubles and storing them in some rental locker to be forgotten; it rather comes from the sense of seeing the world around you differently. Imagine you are viewing waves at the beach through a telescopic lens and slowly begin widening the lens, backing the view up, backing away from the waves. The waves are still there, but now the view contains much more. More sand, of course, but perhaps now too, beach blankets, umbrellas, running children, and sand dunes. The waves continue coming ashore, smoothing the sand and retreating, but there is more in the picture now. There is greater awareness; life is more than waves crashing ashore.

This greater awareness of the world surrounding us comes with a sense of belonging to something greater than just ourselves and just the situation at hand. Imagine if, instead of the waves crashing ashore, the scene you are watching through the telescopic lens is a headache crashing ahead. The wider we can explore the headache, the more we may be able to understand it as a part of us that ebbs and flows like the tides. Probing the headache, being mindful of the headache, and not trying to just box it up and send it to storage with aspirin, may help us understand that this headache is just one part of us, one part of the wide vast world in the lens, and with enough practice, perhaps we will experience pain reduction.

After surviving Nazi concentration camps during World War II, Victor Frankel wrote *Man's Search for Meaning*. In it, he explains that while we cannot avoid suffering in our lives, we can choose how we deal with it. Choosing our responses instead of just reacting is the key. We can only choose a response if we take the time to consider possible choices, and we can only consider choices if we are alert, awake, and aware (piloting) instead of cruising unconsciously on autopilot.

Actively piloting often provides us with opportunities to become aware of so much more of what is going on in addition to whatever our neural system automatically programmed into our autopilot. Anyone who has driven a car with a manual transmission can immediately relate because driving a manual transmission requires more attention. We tune into and rely on the sounds of the engine and the feel of the transmission to know when it is appropriate to shift gears. Automatic transmissions do this, well, automatically—without us thinking, without us paying attention. While I am not advocating that everyone should drive only manual transmissions, I am saying that driving a manual transmission from time to time can provide an opportunity to appreciate driving on another level. I, for one, feel closer to the road and to the driving experience when I have a third pedal. It doesn't matter whether I am on my way to the beach or along a winding road through a forest. And it is true that people who drive manual transmission can become experts and reduce their attention on the process but there is still a part of them that remains aware of the sounds of the engine and feel of the transmission.

As we pay attention to what we are doing as we are doing it, we increase the opportunity to tune into the greater world around us. And as we develop the habit to become more aware of the present moment, we develop a sense of space in the world around us, and within this space often lies the possibility to respond to the world around us instead of mindlessly reacting to it. It is not just that paying more attention to driving makes us less prone to accidents, which it does, it is that by paying attention to our driving, by hearing the car engine, by feeling the sense of motion, by noticing the sky, the lights, and the cars around us, we gain a sense of being more than a law student with too much to do and too little time to do it in. And as we pay attention to (focus on) eating lunch, washing dishes, showering, preparing for crim law, etc., we gain a sense of being more than *just another law student going through her day*. We become more aware of who we are and where we are in our day. This greater sense of self gives us a greater sense of space, and in this greater sense of space, there often arises an opportunity to take time to respond to life around us instead of immediately mindlessly reacting to what occurs. While split-second, near-unconscious reactions taken to avoid traffic accidents are welcome in emergencies, most of the time we spend behind the wheel does not involve reacting to emergencies; the same is true for most of the time we spend behind the wheel of life—emergencies occur infrequently. This means that most often as we move through life, we have the opportunity to reflect and respond to stimuli and situations presented to us instead of just reacting and mindlessly jumping right in. Most often, however, we automatically react—often overreact—to situations as they arise.

The more moments you pay attention to the moment, the more often you will remember that you have the ability to respond instead of reacting. Even as your spine crawls after hearing Professor Intimidation call your name and you feel the eyes of your classmates on you. The jolt of panic is real, it is not going to magically disappear. However, the more moments you have practiced living in the moment, the more likely you are to remember three things: that you have a breath, that it is your breath, and that you never need anyone's permission to take a breath. (Or two or three.) Even Professor Intimidation will wait as you pause, breathe, and formulate your answer. (After all, you did read and prepare the material last night, right?) Mindfulness is not about making stress or unpleasantries go away, but it does help us begin to see them in a new light; it helps us relate to them differently. Mindfulness helps us remember that we are more than what is unfolding at the moment; we are more than our skin crawling, more than just having just heard our name called. Yes, Professor Intimidation is still there, and she is still waiting for your answer, but this is what Professor Intimidation does to everyone. She calls on them and intimidates them; it's just your turn. No bigee. You read the case, you understand the case, and after gathering yourself together during a one- or two-breath pause, you begin your answer. You are still self-conscious and nervous, but the fear is diminished because you remembered to pause and take a few breaths to remind yourself, *I got this.*

Mindful Intentional Piloting and Mindless Autopiloting

> *When you step into the Now, you step out of the content of your mind. The incessant stream of thinking slows down. Thoughts don't absorb all your attention anymore, don't draw you in totally. Gaps arise in between thoughts-spaciousness, stillness. You begin to realize how much vaster and deeper you are than your thoughts.* – Eckhart Tolle

We need and use both intentional and mindless piloting options every day. Numbingly rote routines certainly lend themselves to being outsourced by the unconscious pilot. Why waste time and precious brain power focusing on minor routines in life? Just toss on some clothes, lace up your shoes, and get out for a jog. Any musician will tell you that muscle memory allows them to play their music. They no longer read and play the music note-by-note, although early on it is likely they did. Reading music is the same as reading words; when you memorize a poem or a musical riff, you play from memory without stopping at each note or word. Do you remember when you began learning to read? Do you remember how slowwwwwwwly you moved from word to word and almost letter by letter on the bigger words you needed to sound out? You probably even slid your finger across the page. Stopping at every word at first, your finger picking up speed until you eventually slid your finger over the page, gliding it fluidly over the line of text. And then suddenly, someone—it was my mom for me—decided that I didn't need my finger to read anymore, that my finger was slowing my reading down. Of course, Mom was right again. Her thinking seemed counterintuitive at first because without my finger crutch my reading slowed before eventually picking back up and taking off ever more quickly. I bet that you almost always read aloud when you first started reading and that when you learned to read silently, you still heard your voice narrating inside your head. (It's okay if you still hear yourself narrating when you read silently today, many people still do.)

You are a good reader; you couldn't make it to law school without being a good reader. We are such great readers that our minds no longer stop at every word, in fact, we often clump words together as we read, and our minds fill in blanks for us. And because we have read as much as we have, we have learned patterns, and our minds fill in any missing gaps based upon our years of reading. As an example, I bet you can identify these two Broadway plays even without their vowels.

Th Phntm f th pr[11]

[11] Phantom of the Opera

Jss Chrst Sprstr[12]

Or what about these animals after disemvoweling?

Tgr[13]

Lbstr[14]

Lphnt[15]

Pngn[16]

Dlphn[17]

Grff[18]

I remind all my students, just as I reminded you, that they are good readers. And I point out how our minds clump words together to fill in missing gaps based on our years of reading. However, I also point out the dangers of reading in clumps and automatically guessing when filling in missing gaps. Many common English words—thank goodness the use of law Latin has pretty much atrophied—take on special meanings and relationships in law. Do you remember the first time you encountered the word "reasonable" in a law school classroom? The problem with automatically and unconsciously filling in the gaps is that we might miss something. Your reading probably slowed way down when you began reading cases for the first time, may have made you feel like you felt when Mom first disallowed your finger. Case law, statutes and regulations make for thick and chewy reading; they don't read like a novel at the beach. I recommend my students to slow down their reading at

---

12 Jesus Chris Superstar

13 Tiger

14 Lobster

15 Elephant

16 Penguin

17 Dolphin

18 Giraffe

first because many of them will automatically, unknowingly, unconsciously, and erroneously fill in too many gaps.

I know this because too many students who may believe they have prepared for class cannot accurately tell me what a court held in the case under discussion. I understand there may be gaps in understanding the court's reasoning and knowing how and why the court wound up where it did—that's what the class conversation is about—but for us to have any meaningful conversation about the case, we need to agree on where the court winds up. For example, did the court find adverse possession or not? Were there minimum contacts or not? Was the defendant found guilty or innocent? Not only are students muddled about where the court winds up (which is okay because you are a student), but far too often, students report a case result that is the complete opposite of what the court held! In essence, they tell me that Romeo and Juliet lived happily ever after and had two kids, a dog, and a cat! As far as I can tell, the two most likely reasons for getting the case backwards are that the student never read the case, or that the student read the case so quickly and superficially that they missed the entire story.

There is nothing inherently wrong about reading, writing, or anything else(ing) on autopilot, it is just that we too regularly (most of the time) cruise on autopilot for everything we do. *It's 2 am, just 35 more pages to read for Ahlers; let's plow through them in the next twenty minutes!* When we are on autopilot, it is as if we are skimming through life instead of diving in. And as we absentmindedly skim by, we pass up opportunities to create spaces and pauses for us to consider different responses instead of merely reacting. And who couldn't use a pause or a bit of space now and again? Like when we are freaking out about final exams. . . and it is only the first week of classes. Like when we disagree in a big way with our favorite person. . . just before we leave for campus. Like when we finally need to muster the courage to tell Mom to back off.

Like when our adorable puppy gets sick and needs to go to the vet. Like when our adorable human puppy begins acting far from adorable and needs to go to bed.

Driving Past Our Exit

I remember driving home one time from the beach with four of my children. It had been a great day. We were happy, tired, hungry, and headed for one of our favorite restaurants to enjoy some Rock Shrimp and hush puppies. The music and conversation were lively while I kept counting down the green mileage markers on the side of the Interstate. Fifteen miles to our exit. Ten. Five. And the next thing I know, we were seven miles past our exit! I was shocked when I saw the latest milepost and thought how odd that they misnumbered the mile marker. It took me a few seconds to realize that that was not what happened; we simply overshot our exit. And I thought I was paying attention! I certainly meant to pay attention and had been paying attention up to some point in time. It was a spooky feeling, almost as if I just woke up. I hadn't fallen asleep or anything, but suddenly I was a good chunk of the highway past the restaurant. How had I dropped the ball? When did I stop paying attention to the mile markers? The music and happy conversation in the car took over, but to this day, I still wonder where my mind went instead of focusing on the mile markers.

A friend and colleague of mine who also teaches mindfulness, Professor Katerina Lewinbuk, talks about driving home from campus one afternoon. Thoughts of a faculty meeting that just ended played and replayed repeatedly in her mind as she drove home. Professor Lewinbuk told me about being surprised when she pulled into her driveway. "I was completely oblivious to the drive. It's as if I woke up in my driveway. I couldn't tell you which route I took home."

When our minds are already occupied, which is often, life passes us by without us noticing because we are busy noticing whatever movie is playing in our head instead of noticing the present moment. We miss a wonderful dinner and time spent with loved ones because we are thinking about last semester's grades or thinking about tomorrow's civ pro class. We miss a good movie on Netflix and snuggling with our favorite person because we are worried about upcoming finals—still two months away—or worried about our pet who has to go to the vet tomorrow. Or simply because of the magnetic draw of the handheld portal-to-anywhere-but-here. Being preoccupied means we are already occupied by something or somewhere else, not what is unfolding in front of us. And while we are living the thoughts inside our heads, we can miss more than our exit; we can miss opportunities to fully appreciate all that we have and all that is going on. The mind being preoccupied and full is why Eckhart Tolle believes the word mind*ful*ness is inaccurate. While mindfulness practices are not meant to empty our minds, they certainly can help give us a sense of greater space and perhaps a sense of slowing the pace of our thoughts.

Giving Priority to Whatever Is Occurring in the Present Moment

> *Realize deeply that the present moment is all you have. Make the now the primary focus of your life.* —Eckhart Tolle

This is a great boiled-down explanation of mindfulness. The more time we spend focusing on what is occurring in the moment, the more alert we will be and the less time we will spend creating thoughts of fear and anxiety of yesterdays and tomorrows and stirring the fears into turmoil and unease.

But why should I pay attention while washing the bleeping dishes again, you may ask. They are never done; there are always more dishes to wash! And then there is laundry; I don't enjoy doing laundry either you might add. Why should I pay attention to folding and putting things away? And I don't like that I tore my meniscus and am using crutches; why should I focus on that pain in my uh, knee?

It is true that we would rather pay attention to the more pleasant moments of life and either ignore, numb, or fast forward through the less fun moments. I mean, why pay attention to sitting in the dentist's chair? I just want him to be done! One reason to practice giving priority to what is presently happening is to develop the skill to focus on whatever confronts you, good, bad, or ugly. When you practice paying attention to what is happening, you develop a way of seeing things unfold in more space and time. You begin to see and appreciate that there is more to the present moment than a quick glance captures; there is more to you and more to your life than the dirty dishes in your sink. There is more to you than your toothache, more to you than laundry needing folding. Yet all of these things are part of your experience.

The more you practice paying attention to the dishes, the laundry, and the dentist, the more you will pay attention to candlelit dinners, Netflix snuggles, and celebrating wins. You will also learn to be focused on the task at hand. Studying property law, perhaps, or answering a sample essay question to help prepare for your wills, trusts, and estate final exam. The more practice you have paying attention, the better you will be able to let the noise go and focus on the task at hand.

Giving priority to what is going on in the moment helps us organize our days and lives. There is no escaping the stress of midterm and final exams. No amount of mindfulness practice will completely dissipate law school stress. (Although sound study skills systematically applied throughout the semester certainly reduce it.) However, regular mindfulness practice does help us develop the ability to experience stress differently. The stress does not magically disappear, but it can become more manageable simply by taking the time to look at it. Acknowledging that we are stressed goes a long way in helping us healthily manage that stress instead of self-medicating and numbing ourselves in hopes that it will go away.

One formal practice that Mindfulness-Based Stress Reduction (MBSR) programs introduce is the body scan which guides students through a thorough, systematic review of what is going on in their bodies at that moment. Regularly conducting body scans helps us learn how to examine what is going on with our bodies, imperfections, pain, and all. Regularly scanning, reviewing, checking in, and inventorying our bodily sensations help us develop a different relationship with pain. Just as exam-induced stress is not eliminated by practicing mindfulness, neither is pain eliminated. We can, however, learn to have a different relationship with pain and with stress by practicing mindfulness. While it may seem counterintuitive to shine a light on our pain—after all, when a child gets hurt, don't we include distraction as part of our attempt to help soothe them?—mindfulness training helps us expand our view and our experience of the pain. In short, we get really curious about the pain and, with enough practice, come to experience the pain separately from our response to the pain.

MBSR

> *Academic pressure tends to affect the mental health of college students negatively. . . MBSR effectively reduced stress scores. . . . Even two months after the training, subjects in the Test group exhibited lower negative emotional states, especially in the Anxiety and Depression scores. . . . In conclusion, the sustained*

effects of MBSR were successfully demonstrated based on the reduction of subjective stress perception score. . . .[19]

MBSR stands for Mindfulness-Based Stress Reduction, an eight-week program pioneered and developed by Jon Kabat-Zinn and colleagues at the University of Massachusetts Medical School Stress Reduction Clinic in 1979. The clinic set out to determine whether practicing mindfulness techniques could improve the health and well-being of patients experiencing chronic pain and serious illness. The classes meet weekly for lessons, discussions, and practice and culminate with a day (six hours) of silent mindfulness practice. It worked. This model has been replicated and is now taught throughout the United States and around the world in hospitals, medical schools, clinics, and online.

Here is the table of contents for the Palouse MBSR course. Each week's lesson consists of videos, readings, formal and informal mindfulness practices, and homework which consists of journaling about the topics of the week and your mindfulness practices.

Week 1: Simple Awareness; Raisin Meditation and the Body Scan

Week 2: Attention and The Brain; Introduction to Sitting Meditation

Week 3: Dealing with Thoughts; Introduction to Yoga

Week 4: Stress: Responding vs. Reacting; STOP: The One-Minute Breathing Space

Week 5: Dealing with Difficult Emotions or Physical Pain; Turning Toward. . .

---

[19] An, Anh et al. *Investigating the Effect of Mindfulness-Based Stress Reduction on Stress Level and Brain Activity of College Students.* IBRO neuroscience reports vol. 12 399-410. 14 May, https://www.ncbi.nlm.nih.gov/pmc/articles/PMC9121238/.

Week 6: Mindfulness and Communication; Lake and Mountain Meditations

Week 7: Mindfulness and Compassion; Lovingkindness and Walking Meditation

Week 8: Conclusion; Developing a practice of your own

The course is self-paced. Students are expected to practice at least six days and feel as if they've "gotten the essence" of the week's lesson before moving to the following week. I'm proud that I finished the course and recommend it to everyone; I am not proud to say it took me over a year to complete the eight weeks.

Non-Judging/Labeling

Mindfulness training talks a lot about non-judging. Much of this lesson is aimed at the propensity we all have to instantly size up—judge—people, places, and situations; to size up everything. To categorize everything instantly and constantly. A stranger we never met enters a room and we immediately begin scrutinizing their—clothing, demeanor, height, weight, and attractiveness to calculate whether we will like them. They haven't crossed the room or opened their mouth yet, but we've already begun our assessment.

We were first taught to sort and label things when we were young. *What animal doesn't belong? Circle tallest tree. Which bird is different?* I remember when I first learned to read that I could not stop automatically reading billboards and signs. Automatically, once the symbols clicked, I couldn't turn them off. We judge, sort, and label almost unconsciously. Mindfulness aims to turn off automatic labeling and judging. Lawyers, of course, are trained to make judgments. We make judgments all the time; where we live, who we date and marry, the car we drive, the law school we attend. Conscious decision making is fine; that is how we make plans and move forward in our lives. It's the unconscious labeling going on underneath our radar that mindfulness exposes. The sense of time and space that practicing mindfulness affords us helps us pause to consider our actions before making knee-jerk decisions, including decisions on strangers.

Beginner's Mind

Think of children. To a child, everything is new and to be explored. Everything they see, taste, touch, smell, or hear. The whole world is to be explored! Their curiosity is piqued by everything. They go from experience to experience patching the world together bit by bit. At some point we lose this natural curiosity, this playful inquisitiveness. A Golden Retriever walks by. We don't really see the dog, as Jon Kabat-Zin described earlier, we just see dogness, okay maybe big dogness in the case of our Golden, but usually all dogs except perhaps our pet, morph into amalgamated dogness.

Viewing the visual arts with a beginner's mind is easy for me because I am not an artist and I have never studied art; visual art awes me. It all is like new to me. I like and enjoy music and my taste in music is eclectic. However, I listen to new music that my children introduce me to with a beginner's mind as well. The reason I approach new music and the visual arts with a beginner's mind is because I am consciously actively trying to see and hear them. Most often in life, however, we do not actively engage, we skim the surface. *Seen one dog, seen them all. Look at that kid. Just another final exam to mess up. Man, that gunner in the front row!*

Mindfulness allows us in our expanded sense of space and time to get to know someone before sizing them up, to listen to and hear what someone is saying instead of anticipating what they will say. Mindfulness can help teach us to listen to someone to hear them instead of formulating a response to the words they haven't yet uttered.

Sprinkling a bit of awe in our days helps us see there may be more to a stranger, to a contract, to opposing council, to the judge, to your boss, to your friends, to your children and spouse, to your neighborhood, to your workplace, and on and on.

PART 2

Why Practice Mindfulness?

We are not troubled by things, but by the opinions we have about things. —Epictetus

Benefits of Practicing Mindfulness

Countless studies provided evidence of the effectiveness of mindfulness training. Here are four examples.

- The U.S. Department of Health and Human Services's National Institutes of Health says that mindfulness-based activities have been shown to reduce anxiety and depression and that there is evidence that mindfulness can lower blood pressure, improve sleep, and help people cope with pain.[1]
- The American Psychological Association says that regular mindfulness practice helps reduce rumination, stress, and emotional reactivity, helps improve focus, working memory, and cognitive

[1] *NIH News in Health*, June 2021, 1, https://newsinhealth.nih.gov/2021/06/mindfulness-your-health.

flexibility including the ability to develop adaptive responses to stressful or negative situations.[2]

- According to the Harvard Medical School, practicing mindfulness increases a sense of well-being, making "it easier to savor the pleasures in life as they occur. . . and creates a greater capacity to deal with adverse events." Harvard reports that scientists discovered mindfulness can "help relieve stress, treat heart disease, lower blood pressure, reduce chronic pain," improve sleep, and that psychotherapists use mindfulness meditation techniques to treat "depression, substance abuse, eating disorders, couples' conflicts, anxiety disorders, and obsessive-compulsive disorder."[3]
- The UKs Mental Health Foundation finds that people who practice mindfulness understand their emotions better, cope better with difficult thoughts, feel calmer, increase their ability to focus, concentrate, and pay attention, and enjoy improved relationships. According to the Foundation, practicing mindfulness "can significantly reduce the symptoms of anxiety and depression. . . and help people who have been depressed several times to stay well and avoid relapsing."[4]

I will stop here, but the list of organizations and scientific studies that identify benefits of practicing mindfulness is almost endless and growing every day. For law students I feel

[2] Daphne Davis and Jeffrey Hayes. *What are the benefits of mindfulness*, *Monitor on Psychology*, v. 43, No. 7 at 64, https://www.apa.org/monitor/2012/07-08/ce-corner.

[3] *Harvard Health. Benefits of Mindfulness*, https://www.helpguide.org/harvard/benefits-of-mindfulness.htm.

[4] https://www.mentalhealth.org.uk/explore-mental-health/a-z-topics/mindfulness.

the greatest benefits to practicing mindfulness techniques include reducing the sense of anxiety and increasing your ability to focus and your overall sense of well-being. The stresses of law school and life continue, but mindfulness allows you the space to create a different relationship with them. Final exams are still final exams, but you gain a new perspective on them. Professor Cold Caller still calls on people out of the blue, but somehow, somewhere deep inside, you realize that you can handle her because she's not the boss of you; you are.

Mindfulness Improves Focus

> *And the faculty of voluntarily bringing back a wandering attention, over and over again, is the very root of judgment, character, and will.* —William James

Ah, the ability to focus! How more efficient we would all be without the distractions and disturbances of the wondering mind. Unfortunately, our minds naturally wander incessantly. Even with our portals-to-everywhere-but-here safely stashed in the other room, we too frequently visit yesterdays, last weeks, and months and years gone by to reopen old wounds, rehash old arguments, retry old wrongs, and revisit old should-have-dones. If not retreating to the past, we escape to the future, to tomorrows, to coming weeks, and to months and years in the future. Escaping ahead, we preheat our oven of anxiety, worries, and fears by imagining worse case scenarios, accepting them as true, and bracing for them. Rarely do we stay present. And that is a shame because the present requires no reopening, rehashing, retrying, nor revisiting. No imagining and accepting the worst. All we need to do is pay attention to the task in front of us.

Regularly practicing mindfulness helps us stay tuned and locked in. Our minds will continue to wander of course—after all, they are incessant, perpetual, unrelenting, dancing, waving, and wriggling thought generators. But with continued practice mindfulness helps us develop the refocus muscle. Our minds may wander, but we return to whatever presently needs to be accomplished. How much and how often do we need to practice? Most MBSR courses suggest minimum 20- to 30-minute formal meditations daily and as many micro-meditations throughout each day as possible. Jon Kabat-Zins program requires patients to meditate 45 minutes daily.

That amount of time often seems frightening and undoable to newcomers, so I recommend beginners start out meditating as few as two or three minutes daily, eventually building to 5, 10, 15, 20 minutes, and more. Finding 20 minutes to eat or sleep or spend time with loved ones is hard enough. Sitting quietly seemingly "doing nothing" seems waste of time, but to some, spending time at the gym seems a waste of time—to those who do not care to work out. Those of us who exercise know we miss it when we skip it. Like anything in life, once something becomes a habit (good or bad), you don't want to do without it. Twenty-minute meditations were tough for me once upon a time, but now that I have experienced the physical, mental, and emotional benefits, I rarely miss meditating at least 20 minutes each day.

But don't let the numbers scare you. Do what you can. Daily 5-minute meditations will help. Don't be surprised, however, if after establishing your daily 5-minute routine that the number of minutes begins to grow as you become more familiar with the practice and begin to notice the differences practicing mindfulness brings. The calmer you become, the easier it becomes for you to maintain your focus on tonight's reading, for example and not worries about final exams in two months.

Practicing Mindfulness Reduces Anxiety and Increases Calm

In daily life, there is so much to do and so little time. You may feel pressured to run all the time. Just stop! Touch the ground of the present moment deeply, and you will touch real peace and joy. —Thich Nhat Hanh.

The greatest weapon against stress is our ability to choose one thought over another. —William James

I do not have to tell you that law school breeds anxiety. Bloomberg Law reports that most law students struggle with mental health issues because of law school-related issues. Over 75% of the students who responded reported increased anxiety; over 50% reported experiencing depression.[5] Over half acknowledged that their well-being worsened during the fall 2022 semester; 26% felt it significantly worsened.

Focusing on the present moment instead of anticipating future fears or reliving past regrets goes a long way, not only to help us remain focused, but also to help us reduce anxiety. This occurs because as we spend more time in the present, we begin to build a sense of inner stillness and inner space. MBSR programs often include guided lake and mountain meditations; I provide a guided lake meditation below on page 80. Both mediations provide opportunities to explore and gain a sense of inner stillness and space. Stillness below the surface of the lake even as storms pass, stillness in the mass of the mountain as days, nights, seasons, and weather pass.

I remember one time when I was young and there was a great deal of commotion going on in the house. I do not remember the

---

[5] Blaemire, Jessica. *ANALYSIS: Well-Being in Law School—Law Students Aren't OK*, February 3, 2023, https://news.bloomberglaw.com/bloomberg-law-analysis/analysis-well-being-in-law-school-law-students-arent-ok.

specifics, but I remember a lot of activity, a lot of noise, and many family members scurrying about. It was probably around the holidays. I asked my mother who, no matter the circumstances, never seemed to get bothered. After dodging the crazy storm of activity for a while I asked my mother how she remained calm. "It's easy," she said. "I just choose to remain in the eye of the storm, not flailing around in its winds."

Practicing mindfulness techniques helps us stay in the eye of the storms. We can see, acknowledge, and appreciate the tossing storms in our lives and realize that we are more than the prevailing winds. We come to appreciate that all storms pass, the sun always rises, and new doors open.

Your Amygdala and Sabre-Toothed Tigers

Whenever we see, hear, touch, or taste something, sensory information is directed to our thalamus. When faced with a threatening situation, the thalamus sends sensory information to both the amygdala (emotional brain) and the neocortex (thinking brain). When our amygdala senses danger, it makes a split-second decision to initiate a fight-or-flight response which releases stress hormones, including adrenaline and cortisol, among others, to prepare us to fight or flee. Our blood pressure shoots up, our heart pumps faster, and our energy increases.

These responses, appropriate millions of years ago while we lived on the savannah where turning any corner could bring us face to face with a Sabre-Toothed Tiger and immediate peril to our lives, are less appropriate today. In this century, having largely left the savannah behind, most of us have not, do not, and will not face the decision to fight or flee a Sabre-Toothed Tiger.

Having said that, we all know people who turn everything into a potential disaster—*I'll never pass this class*! *I'll never get a date with her! She will never help me with this!*—Most of what occurs to us, however, is not an emergency although our automatic reactions do not know this and react as if emergencies abound.

Unfortunately, our brains haven't evolved as fast as the rest of us has evolved and our body still releases its hormonal cocktail to prepare us for fight or flight even though Sabre-Toothed Tigers are long extinct.

Cell Phone and Internet Addictions

> Your phone can be anything—including a grenade, its target the cohesion and integrity of your thoughts. For almost anyone who owns one, a smartphone is not only the most omnipresent distraction from a mindfulness practice; it's also most likely a principal vector for much of the stuff that unfocuses, stresses, addicts, enrages, or dismays you. —Michael Owen[6]

> *I went to the woods because I wished to live deliberately.*
> —Henry David Thoreau

If there is such a thing as the opposite of living deliberately, I suspect it looks something like students crossing campus, heads buried in their portals, never looking up. Readers already know what I think about our palm-held portals-to-anywhere-but-here. They are Trouble. I know how long and hard I tried to find ways to slow things down in my life, and yes, perhaps a bit of an escape from the pace of the world. My quest started last century when books like Alvin Toffler's 1970 *Future Shock* were best sellers. Future shock is defined as a "condition of distress and disorientation brought on by the inability to cope with rapid societal and technological change."[7]

---

6 Michael Owen. *Your Phone Is a Mindfulness Trap, The Atlantic*, June 23, 2023, https://www.theatlantic.com/health/archive/2023/06/meditation-app-mind-distraction/674500/.

7 The American Heritage Dictionary of the English Language, 5th Edition.

There were many rapid societal and technological changes occurring in the United States in the 1960s. Many of us longed to slow things down, to "go up the country," as Canned Heat sang at Woodstock in 1969: "I'm gonna leave this city, got to get away/ All this fussing and fighting, man, you know I sure can't stay.[8]

And yes, maybe the hippies were after a bit of slowing down, a bit of escapism; maybe Thoreau was too during his two-year foray to Walden Pond. Thoreau and the hippies didn't have access to handy portals-to-anywhere-but-here. Neither did Christ or Buddha, as we discussed above. Buddha, Christ, Thoreau, and the hippies were all looking for ways to deal with life way before the handheld portals that steal you away from paying attention.

Our phones are useful; my portable calendar was invaluable when I was Associate Dean. I needed to know when and where I needed to be, and its instant updates were indispensable. As a tool it's cool. My phone is not much of a plaything for me (although I may have to admit to a slight addiction to Sudoku). I, author and teacher of mindfulness, also occasionally catch myself spilling precious time down some rabbit hole to anywhere but here suggested by my news feed, ugh! My phone, however, doesn't sleep beside me; it charges in the kitchen. And it is not the first thing I reach for in the mornings. It may be among the first ten things, but I am not in a rush to watch a cute cat video, see if my crush responded to my most recent flirt, or learn what the weather is like. It's Florida. It's hot.

Top excuses my students give me for sleeping with their phones include, *someone may have an emergency, my friend Mary is going through a rough patch right now, I don't have an alarm clock, I might not hear it ring in the kitchen, I'm waiting to hear back from my so-and-so.* (Always makes me wonder how many years they are

---

[8] Canned Heat. *Going Up the Country*, from *Living the Blues* (Liberty Records, 1968).

going to continue waiting to hear back from so-and-so.) I tell them that my lay opinion is that they are addicted because why otherwise would their separation anxiety be so great—especially when we are talking about charging the phone in another room during a time when presumably they won't need it because they are sleeping. I might charge my phone on the bedstand only when something important is going on that might necessitate me responding in a hurry if the phone rang in the middle of the night. (I do not recall ever doing this, but I can imagine that I might.) Otherwise, as I've taught my children, phones have no constitutional right to be answered. When I wanted alone time back in the days when phones were attached to walls, I left my phone off the hook or unplugged it so it wouldn't ring and disturb me. My friends occasionally took issue with this, but they knew what my answer would be—no constitutional right to be answered.

One of my children recently met up with buddies in New York. While recounting their tales they sang the praises of their cell phones for saving them when the group got separated on the subway and asked me how my friends and I navigated the city without phones back in the day. "What if you got separated, how did you ever find each other," they asked. I told them it was simple, first; we didn't get on a train unless we all got on the train, second, if we did get separated—it happened—we knew to meet at a certain location where everyone would wait until we all had arrived. It's not rocket science. Cell phones are remarkable tools but have evolved into magnets dragging us to endless anywheres and anytimes other than here and now. I encourage my students to just explore their portal usage and think about ways to maybe bring it down a notch or two. Here are some tips.

1. I already mentioned my first suggestion for gaining a little breathing room around our portal usage: charge the phone in another room overnight. If you

use it as your morning alarm, buy an alarm clock and use it instead.

2. Do not use your phone first thing in the morning. Do anything before reaching for your phone. This is easier done if the phone is in another room. For example, say hello to pets and people in the home, brush your teeth, wash your face, have a cup of coffee, eat breakfast, lay out your clothes, meditate, anything but reach for your phone.

3. Keep in mind the toddler's rule, out of sight, out of mind. Keep your phone in your pocket, your purse, your backpack, or in your car; keep it out of sight. Research shows your ability to think drops markedly when your phone is within reach, even if silenced or turned off.

4. When you are studying, leave the portal in another room. Some students tell me it is their timer. If they can't hear the phone's timer in another room, I suggest they use the microwave or oven, timer; they're usually loud enough to hear throughout the house. Alexa and Google Assistant will also cheerfully keep timers.

5. Get out of the phone (talking is okay) 30 minutes before you go to bed. If you like to read yourself to sleep, use a good book instead and avoid the blue light of the portal which only serves to wake you up.

6. Consider a portal curfew. Tell family, friends, and study buddies to contact you only for emergencies after whatever time you feel is appropriate (11 p.m.?)

7. Schedule time to play Sudoku, chase chats, and fall into rabbit holes—set a timer and stick to the schedule.

Because You Are Stressed out

> *96% of law students experience significant stress, compared to 70% of med students and 43% of grad students.*[9]

As I mentioned in the beginning, research shows that law students suffer from higher levels of stress than other postgraduate students, and you know perhaps better than I that law students often turn to alcohol, drugs, and other unhealthy habits in hopes of alleviating the pressure of law school. Most law students live "unbalanced" lives strung along by caffeine, late nights, ignoring loved ones, and going full Shrek, stay-out-of-my-swamp mode weeks at a time before final exams. And in between full-out Shrek modes, finding a balance is simply not a priority for most.

While practicing mindfulness does not put an end to reading, exams, project deadlines, health issues, bills, oil changes, trips to the vet, laundry, shopping, dirty dishes, disagreements at home, in-laws, and unpleasant surprises, it can help.

Three studies help assess the situation.

A 2014 Survey of Law Student Well-Being reported that of students enrolled in fifteen law schools, 17% suffered from depression, 37% experienced anxiety, 6% entertained suicidal thoughts, and that 25% were at risk of becoming alcoholics.[10]

---

[9] The Full Weight of Law School: Stress on Law Students is Different. *Lawyer Well-Being & Mental Health, Massachusetts LAP Blog*, January 18, 2019, https://www.lclma.org/2019/01/18/the-full-weight-of-law-school-stress-on-law-students-is-different/.

[10] Jerome M. Organ, David B. Jaffe, and Kathryn M. Bender, *Suffering in Silence: The Survey of Law Student Well-Being and the Reluctance of Law Students to Seek Help for Substance Use and Mental Health Concerns*, 66 *J. Legal Educ.* 116 (2016).

In 2016, an ABA and Hazelden Betty Ford Foundation study found that nearly a quarter to one-third of practitioners qualify as problem drinkers, 28% struggle with depression, 19% struggle with anxiety, and 23% struggle with levels of stress.[11]

A 2017 Harvard Law School student government survey found that 24% of Harvard law students reported anxiety, 25% reported depression, and 20.5% were at heightened suicide risk. 66% reported new mental health challenges since beginning law school.[12]

The National Task Force on Lawyer Well-Being, created in 2016 in large part to address the concerns raised by the 2014 and 2016 studies, released its report, *The Path to Lawyer Well-Being: Practical Recommendations for Positive Change* in 2017.

To be a good lawyer, one has to be a healthy lawyer. Sadly, our profession is falling short when it comes to well-being. The two studies referenced above reveal that too many lawyers and law students experience chronic stress and high rates of depression and substance use. These findings are incompatible with a sustainable legal profession, and they raise troubling implications for many lawyers' basic competence. This research suggests that the current state of lawyers' health cannot support a profession dedicated to client service and dependent on the public trust.[13]

Among other things, the report makes recommendations to eliminate the stigma associated with help-seeking behaviors, to emphasize well-being as an indispensable part of lawyer competence, and to educate lawyers, judges, and law students on lawyer well-being issues.

---

[11] Patrick R. Krill, Ryan Johnson, and Linda Albert, *The Prevalence of Substance Use and Other Mental Health Concerns Among American Attorneys*, 10 J. *Addiction Med.* 46 (2016).

[12] Amanda Chan, Amanda Lee, and Adam Savitt, *Wellness at the Law School: Promises to Keep and Miles to Go Before We Sleep, Harv. Crimson*, Mar. 28, 2018.

[13] National Task Force On Lawyer Well-Being, *The Path to Lawyer Well-Being: Practical Recommendations for Positive Change* (The Task Force 2017).

These are bold steps forward. The American Bar Association and State Bar associations have established many pathways to help attorneys in need of assistance instead of fearing reprisal or worrying about the negative impact of seeking help with difficulties. It is important to note that law students are included in the messaging and are encouraged to seek help before the wheels come off the tracks.

One educational lesson suggested by the report is mindfulness meditation.[14]

> Mindfulness meditation is a practice that can enhance cognitive reframing (and thus resilience) by aiding our ability to monitor our thoughts and avoid becoming emotionally overwhelmed. A rapidly growing body of research on meditation has shown its potential for help in addressing a variety of psychological and psychosomatic disorders, especially those in which stress plays a causal role.[15] One type of meditative practice is mindfulness—a technique that cultivates the skill of being present by focusing attention on your breath and detaching from your thoughts or feelings. Research has found that mindfulness can reduce rumination, stress, depression, and anxiety.[16] It also can enhance a host of competencies related to lawyer effectiveness, including increased focus and concentration, working memory, critical cognitive skills, reduced burnout, and ethical and rational decision-

[14] The Report, Appendix B.

[15] R. Walsh & S. L. Shapiro (2006), *The Meeting of Meditative Disciplines and Western Psychology*, 61 *AM. PSYCHOL.* 227 (2006).

[16] E.g., S. G. Hoffman, A. T. Sawyer, A. A. Witt, & D. Oh, *The Effect of Mindfulness-Based Therapy on Anxiety and Depression: A Meta-Analytic Review*, 78 J. *CONSULTING & CLINICAL PSYCHOL.* 169 (2010); R. Teper, Z. V. Segal, & M. Inzlicht, *Inside the Mindful Mind: How Mindfulness Enhances Emotion Regulation Through Improvements in Executive Control*, 22 *CURRENT DIRECTIONS IN PSYCHOL. SCI.* 449.

making.[17] Multiple articles have advocated for mindfulness as an important practice for lawyers and law students.[18] Evidence also suggests that mindfulness can enhance the sense of work-life balance by reducing workers' preoccupation with work.[19]

I know that I am not telling you anything new when I say the stress of law school is real. Stress is an integral part of life; it is not something that goes away. Like everything else in life, however, it is something that can be managed well or managed poorly. Practicing mindfulness is one way to help you find and maintain, if not equilibrium, at least a manageable route through the extremely stress-filled life the study and practice of law is. What does it mean to practice mindfulness? Let us take a look.

---

[17] A. P. Jha, E. A. Stanley, W. L. Kiyonaga, & L. Gelfand, *Examining the Protective Effects of Mindfulness Training on Working Memory Capacity and Affective Experience*, 10 *EMOTION* 56 (2010); D. Levy, J. Wobbrock, A. W. Kaszniak, & M. Ostergren, *The Effects of Mindfulness Meditation Training on Multitasking in a High-Stress Environment, Proceedings of Graphics Interface Conference* (2012), available at http://faculty.washington.edu/wobbrock/pubs/gi-12.02.pdf; M. D. Mrazek, M. S. Franklin, D. T. Phillips, B. Baird, & J. W. Schooler, *Mindfulness Training Improves Working Memory Capacity and GRE Performance While Reducing Mind Wandering*, 24 *PSYCHOL. SCI.* 776 (2013); N.E. Ruedy & M. E. Schweizer, *In the Moment: The Effect of Mindfulness on Ethical Decision Making*, 95 *J. BUS. ETHICS* 73 (2010); F. Zeidan, S. K. Johnson, B. J. Diamond, Z. David, & P. Goolkasian, *Mindfulness Meditation Improves Cognition: Evidence of Brief Mental Training*, 19 *CONSCIOUSNESS & COGNITION* 597 (2010).

[18] E.g., W. S. Blatt, *What's Special About Meditation? Contemplative Practice for American Lawyers*, 7 *HARV. NEGOT. L. REV.* 125 (2002); Peter H. Huang, *How Improving Decision-Making and Mindfulness Can Improve Legal Ethics and Professionalism*, 21 J. *L. BUS. & ETHICS* 35 (2014).

[19] A. Michel, C. Bosch, & M. Rexroth, *Mindfulness as a Cognitive-Emotional Segmentation Strategy: An Intervention Promoting Work-Life Balance*, 87 *J. OCCUPATIONAL & ORGANIZATIONAL PSYCHOL.* 733 (2014).

PART 3

Practicing Mindfulness

Stand still. The trees ahead and the bushes beside you Are not lost. Wherever you are is called Here, And you must treat it as a powerful stranger, Must ask permission to know it and be known. The forest breathes. Listen. It answers. . . . —David Wagoner

We practice mindfulness formally and informally. Think of formal practices as time specifically set aside; like any good exercise regime, a daily (or almost daily) regular, dedicated time set aside works best for formal practice. Informal exercises are more impromptu and are available literally every moment we are awake. Do not be fooled by their name, informal mindfulness practices are just as important and valuable as formal exercises.

Formal Meditation Practices

Being aware of your breath forces you into the present moment—the key to all inner transformation. Whenever you are conscious of the breath, you are absolutely present. You may also notice that you cannot think and

be aware of your breathing. Conscious breathing stops your mind. —Eckhart Tolle

A Sitting Meditation Focusing on the Breath

The first formal meditation practice we explore is sitting meditation. Regular 5-, 10-, 15- or 20-minute and longer mediations help reinforce the ability to observe without interacting with what is unfolding. Students can begin sitting meditations immediately because they only need a seat and maybe a timer, or they may choose guided meditations. There are countless examples of sitting mediations on the internet. I recommend guided meditations in the beginning.[1] If not using guided meditations, I suggest new mediators begin with short 3- to 5-minute sessions in the beginning and gradually building up.

Any comfortable seat may do. You do not need to sit on the floor in the lotus position. You do not need a yoga mat or a meditation seat, or a cushion. Of course, feel free to sit on the floor, or anywhere else you may sit without slouching or leaning back if possible. Any kitchen or classroom chair will work, as well as any sofa, or an upholstered chair. Unless you are on the floor, we are looking for a comfortable seat that allows you to place your feet flat on the floor and the rest of your body straight.

As we prepare to sit for our meditation, we know we are about to allow ourselves a pause from our incessant moving, doing, and reacting and instead simply pay attention to what is happening within our own awareness right here and now.

You want to sit up straight, not military rigid straight, but sitting like an adult, without slouching. And you want to sit still, not squirming and wiggling like a child. It is best if your back is not

[1] My favorite is from the Palouse Mindfulness course. https://palousemindfulness.com/meditations/sittingmeditation.html.

leaning against the chair. You want your head to be centered, level, and balanced on your shoulders, with your arms and hands resting comfortably, usually in your lap or on your thighs. If you were not reading this, you might close your eyes or focus them in a soft gaze a few feet away.

As you settle in, begin noticing that you are breathing. This may sound funny, but unless you are an athlete, or are currently involved in a strenuous physical activity—which you are not because you are sitting in a chair—you rarely notice the 17,000 daily breaths you take.[2] But that is exactly what you are going to do now. As you sit, notice where you feel your breath. Your nose, your chest, your belly? Do you feel your breath in your nostrils? Is it warm? Cool? Moist or dry? Notice how your belly fills up and expands on each breath in and deflates on each breath out. Do you notice that even your chest and shoulders rise and fall slightly as you breathe?

Focus on the in-and-out rhythm of the entire breath cycle wherever it catches your attention. It varies for me. Sometimes I notice the air in my nose, sometimes I feel my belly puff up and deflate, other times it feels as if all my breathing is going on in my chest. Regardless of where you feel it right now, do you notice the pauses in your breath at either end of the cycle? Notice the stopping points between breathing in and breathing out? When you notice these pauses, you come closer to noticing the entire breath cycle. In and out, pauses and all, we never stop breathing. You might also notice a desire to want to control your breathing, but there is no reason to control it. You've been breathing just fine all day today without thinking about it. There is no need to change your breathing now just because you are focused on it. You are breathing perfectly well, just as your body needs. Breathing in and out.

---

[2] According to the American Lung Association. https://www.lung.org/blog/how-your-lungs-work.

The focus on your breath is gentle, skirting, fleeting. You are just noticing your breath, not scrutinizing, weighing, measuring, or altering it. Think of your breath as yourself on a float in a lake after a boat passes by. Your float gently bobs on the passing wake. You don't measure the timing of the ups and downs or try to alter them; you simply ride them.

As you ride your breath, no matter how vigilant you are, your attention will wander, shifting your focus away from your breath to somewhere else. To worries, memories, fantasies, or to-do lists, perhaps. Wandering is natural. When you finally realize that your focus has changed, you need not feel bad or give yourself a hard time. When you do notice that your mind has wandered, lightly notice where it wandered off to before letting go of the thought and return to focusing on your breath. Just gently bring your awareness back to the physical sensations of breathing, of air moving in and out of your body. Of you on your float in the lake.

Noise may also lure you away from your raft. You may notice sounds in your vicinity that pull your attention away from your breath to the sound. When sound distracts you and pulls your attention away, the goal is to try to experience the sound vibrations as they hit your eardrums without labeling them. Instead of identifying sounds as cars, planes, voices, air conditioning units, or footsteps, just listen to the pitch, rhythm, and intensity of the sounds without automatically slapping labels on them. Listen to the sound just long enough to hear its qualities before returning to your breath. *I hear a sound. Is it loud or soft? High-pitched or low? Pleasing or discordant?* Do not try to label the sound, although do not be disappointed if you automatically label the sound as traffic, music, voices, or a fire engine, for example, that is what our minds do. Once you've noticed that you are listening to a sound rather than paying attention to your breath, just bring your attention back to feeling your breath.

Sometimes you may notice that your mind has wandered onto an opinion you have about something or someone, perhaps liking or not liking the way things are going. Just becoming aware that you have an opinion is powerful in and of itself. Whether your opinion registers pleasure or displeasure does not matter, and you need not sort the matter out just now. It may even feel a little freeing. Not having to address or resolve a situation offers you distance and freedom to address possible recourses at the appropriate time. Mindfulness teaches us about the power of awareness. But for now, we just note our opinion and return to the rhythm of our breath. At this moment, as we sit, it doesn't matter if we like or dislike what is going on, noticing we have an opinion is what matters. Sometimes I am actively liking what is going on, and sometimes my critical mind is busy not liking what is happening. During our sitting meditation, it does not matter which mind is presiding; I can sort out whatever needs to be sorted later. Not now during my sitting meditation.

Many beginning meditators beat themselves up and feel they are failing because their minds keep wandering. They do not realize that wandering, realizing that you are wandering, and returning to your breath only to wander off again is exactly the exercise we went to the mindfulness gym for. They are not doing it wrong. The entire cycle of awareness is important, wandering off from breath and coming back. Focusing, noticing we are not focusing, and returning to our focus again and again and again, builds our focusing muscle. That's what the sitting mediation helps us do. Instead of becoming discouraged, you might try having a mini celebration whenever you catch your mind chasing a thought. *Ha! Caught you! Good job, me!*

Guided Meditations

MBSR's Lake Meditation

Guided meditations come in all shapes and sizes. The following read-your-way-through a-meditation is based upon Jon Kabat-Zinn's original Lake meditation from his MBSR classes. Jon's original and many other versions are readily available on the web (just google lake meditation).

This guided meditation offers you an opportunity to relax and create an image of a lake—mine is nestled in a forest—and invites you to explore the richness of the lake and see how it is ever evolving and yet remains the same as it incorporates, reflects, and embodies changing hours, weather, and seasons.

I prefer to lie down for this meditation, although comfortably sitting somewhere should work as well. Wherever you decide to meditate, settle in, wiggle around, get comfortable, and begin by paying attention to how the bed, chair, sofa, or recliner supports you. Feel your head, back, arms, hips, legs, and heels resting on the surface. Once settled and you feel your body on the bed resting, if you weren't reading this book, you would close your eyes and move your attention to your breath. Remember, you need not change your breathing, you are breathing just fine. Feel yourself lying on the bed, whole, complete, and breathing. As you rest there, noticing your breath and feeling your body touching the bed, bring to mind a lake. Perhaps a lake you know. It might be a small or large lake; its depth and shoreline do not matter. It is your lake.

The visual image need not be perfect. Just get a sense of a lake, get a feel for a lake. Imagine the lake as if it were held cupped in the hands of the earth just as you cup water in your hands for a drink. Imagine the lake cupped and held by the earth. It is resting. Can you sense the presence of the lake? With no wind, it seems almost like a mirror, reflecting the sky, clouds, mountains, birds, trees, shadows, and the sun. All that surrounds the lake is reflected in it as if captured. Momentarily the lake holds everything within itself. In time a wind arrives and disturbs the stillness of the mirror distorting its earlier reflections now splintered into sparkling, bobbing, flashes of light seemingly dancing on the tossing surface. Beneath the surface the lake remains calm. In time the wind will pass, and the sun will set. The moon, perhaps it is full, and the stars now light the sky while the lake welcomes and reflects their lights. Nighttime reflections are mostly shadows. And in the winter the surface of the lake freezes. Cold, rigid, and hard on the surface, yet below the ice the lake is alive.

As you rest breathing and bringing the image and sense of the lake alive, see if you can bring the sense of the lake closer and closer to you until you and the lake become inseparable. Not you splashing or swimming in the lake, you feeling like the lake. Feeling its energies and your energies merging as one. As the lake openly receives and accepts what surrounds it, let your heart and mind be openly cradled in awareness and compassion for yourself just as the lake is cradled by the earth. You and the lake are receptive to and reflect all that comes near. Like a lake, at times you may be without disturbance, still, with crystal clear thoughts and reflections. At other times your life's surface may be choppy, your reflections disturbed, and your depths muddied.

As you lie here you might simply observe the slings and arrows of outrageous fortune that your mind concocts and realize those thoughts and feelings are fleeting, as are your impulses and reactions, just like the effect of the lake's ripples which only temporarily change reflections in the lake. You may also come to appreciate that no matter how large a squall arrives at your lake, no matter how rippled the surface becomes, below the surface, the lake remains calm. Below the ice of winter, fish swim and grasses grow. You may come to realize that squalls, summers, winters, days, and nights, all come and go. Just as your thoughts and emotions come and go. Storms blow through our lives, but if we take the time, we may find that there is more depth; we are more than just a choppy surface. We are so much more. We may be upset with someone or at a situation, but beneath the upset, beneath the surface of the storm, we remain calm because we are cradled in the knowledge that we are far more than a passing storm. We are a reservoir of awareness ready to experience our own storms as well as moments of peace.

Professor Ahlers's Lake Meditation

I wrote this guided meditation to offer a short, refreshing respite from the world. I want to offer a relaxing place to go instead of a hidden, tortured, twisted trail down some newsfeed rabbit hole from which you eventually surface exhausted. Something different than watching more cute cat videos, checking in with the latest drama of the week, or becoming jealous of the vacation photos your friends post on Facebook. I read a version of this during my class.

This guided meditation is meant to offer a brief respite from the world; as we participate, the Earth will continue to rotate without our assistance, and the skies will await our return.

When you are ready, settle in and make yourself comfortable.

Stretch, wiggle, relax, and settle in.

When you are ready, take a deep breath and close your eyes on the exhale. Take another deep breath and feel yourself relax on the exhale.

Returning to normal breathing.

Relaxing even more.

Sitting. . . relaxing. . . breathing. . . nothing to do but notice your breath.

Where do you feel it? Do you feel your breath in your nose. . .? Perhaps in your throat. . .? Perhaps you feel it fill your lungs. . .; perhaps you feel your chest rise, or you feel your belly extend. . . . Just noticing your breath.

Following your breath in; you know it brings you fresh oxygen.

Following your breath out; you know it carries away waste.

Following your breath in. . .and. . .out. . .with each breath, relaxing more. Feeling tension slip away.

Experiencing the power of your breath. Always with us, we take it for granted. . . rarely ever think about it.

Think about it now. Feel your breath energize you with every inhale and feel it relax and cleanse you with every exhale.

Just breathing.

Let the room fade away. Imagine yourself somewhere else. A comfortable place. A theater, perhaps, with dim lights. In front of you is a curtain, and the curtain begins to open.

A show, a show you will create, is about to begin.

Effortlessly, you don't know how, but you find yourself on stage facing two impressive, beautifully carved, polished, and inviting Oak doors.

You know you want to experience what awaits on the other side of the doors. And, as if on cue, your cue, the doors begin, slowly and silently, to swing open towards you, welcoming you with open arms.

Beyond the doors, you see a beautiful, expansive terrain of grasses, trees, and hills bathed in sunshine. In the distance, you see snow-capped mountains. After the doors open completely, you step from the wooden stage onto a soft, lush, carpet of green grass.

Your lungs breathe in the deep, loamy smell of earth. And fresh air tickles your nostrils. You hear songbirds and see colorful, flitting butterflies.

Stepping outside, you notice that there is no weather. It's a no-weather day. The sun is shining, but it isn't blinding. There is no temperature. It isn't cold. It isn't hot. It isn't even warm; the temperature just is. It isn't rainy. It isn't windy. A few, lazy, fluffy, white clouds serenely float by. A perfect no-weather day.

There are only friendly animals here. No stinging or biting insects; any buzz you hear is a cheerful greeting.

You notice a gently sloping path winding through the grasses. You walk leisurely on it, touching and smelling a variety of flowers. Eventually, the path leads to a beach on the shore of a crystalline blue lake. There's a blanket set out and waiting for you, a bathing suit and a towel, and a small pile of perfectly smooth stones calling to be skimmed across the mirror-still surface of the lake.

You sit on the blanket to remove your shoes and find that you're wearing no shoes and that the clothes you were wearing have been replaced by a colorful, stylish, perfectly fitting, and flattering bathing suit.

You pick up several stones from the pile and walk to the lake. You skip the stones effortlessly, expertly, across the surface. Each stone skips five or six times and leaves gentle, growing rings at each skip. You watch the rings expand and disappear. You are at peace.

You pause to drink it all in before sensing that, oh yes, you are going for a swim.

You step into the water and find there is no temperature. The water isn't cold. It isn't hot. It isn't even warm; the temperature just is, a no-temperature lake matching a no-weather day. You wade in stridently. The sand beneath your feet is smooth. In the water, you see fish swimming, darting, their dance seemingly choreographed among undulating plants and grasses.

You walk in chest-deep before taking the plunge. You see perfectly well underwater and find you can breathe. The water is like oxygen. You breathe it in and discover an elixir of hope and vitality. You feel at home playing, swimming, and diving among the colorful fish and aquatic life.

You feel a deep sense of peace and calm as the playful fish and other lake friends swim, dart, frolic, and dance with you.

After a while, you think of the waiting blanket and towel and swim back towards shore. When you get close enough to stand, you walk to the blanket and lie down on your back, watching the blue skies, the occasional cloud, and the friendly birds and insects. Comfortable and calm, you fall into a slight, pleasant, near-sleep as happy insects softly hum by. You are completely at peace.

Time passes as you take it all in. No need to do anything. No deadlines. No have tos. No musts. Just a beautiful, no-weather day to lay on your back and watch clouds. You haven't laid on your back to watch clouds since you were a child.

Eventually you roll over and lean on your elbows. You spot a tall, tall, tree across the lake. You wonder how tall it must be for you to see it at this distance. Really tall, you guess. And as you wonder, you don't know how, but you suddenly find yourself nestled safely among its branches in a large hammock, which you know has been waiting for you.

It is peaceful in the tree. Its limbs, branches, and leaves embrace you. You are up off the ground and perfectly safe. The hammock offers an amazing view. Far away are glaciered mountains. Nearer, are valleys and farms. You see streams and waterfalls. So much to explore!

The birds seem to call you to fly, and once again you don't know how, but you find yourself effortlessly gliding through the skies with perfect ease. You are flying! None of this surprises you. This is your garden, your lake, your place where all is well. A place you can visit whenever you want.

You climb, soar, and spin accompanied by colorful birds. . .

Eventually, completely refreshed, you fly back to the blanket.

When you reach the blanket you are dry and dressed in the clothes you walked in with and you find a basket of fresh, colorful fruit. All your favorite fruits are there, and some you've been wanting to try. You pick a piece of fruit and examine it closely. You feel the weight of it in your hand. You feel its texture. Is it rough, or is it smooth? You bring it up to your nose. . . .

What do you smell? If you need to peel your fruit, do so now. Slowly bring the fruit to your lips and either take a bite or place a piece of it into your open mouth. Roll the food around in your mouth with your tongue. Taste the fruit. You smile because you know this is the best tasting fruit you have had in a long while. Sit awhile to finish and savor your piece of fruit as you soak in the lake and its surroundings. . . .

Relaxed, refreshed, and filled with a great sense of peace, you begin up the path toward the Oak doors.

You step through the doors onto the stage and turn back to look at the lake, knowing you can return whenever you wish.

The doors . . . . slowwwwwwwly . . . .close.

You are back in your seat and begin to become aware of the room.

You notice your breath and become even more aware.

No need to hurry, but when you are ready, gently open your eyes.

Before engaging in your day, take one more deep breath and silently tell yourself, "I am at peace."

Body Scans

Body scans most often address the entire body. Most start either at the feet and move up to the head, or they start and the head and move down. Sometimes they can be used to help address and deal with a specific injury, pain, or physical difficulty. Regularly practicing body scans helps us develop a greater awareness by creating a greater sense of distance from what is unfolding. From this greater distance we create and increase an ability to witness what is unfolding without immediately reacting.

Body scan meditations are usually done lying down, although they need not be. Sitting or reclining works just as well. What is important is that you find a comfortable place; a chair, bed, recliner, or couch is fine, and a time when you won't be interrupted. This generic body scan is based on one from the Palouse Mindfulness-Based Stress Reduction Course.

Lie on your back and rest your arms next to your body. Palms up or down, whichever is more comfortable. Notice your heals on the bed and allow your feet to relax; they may even choose to fall away from each other.

As you are lying here, begin noticing whatever comes up in your awareness. As if you were lying on your back looking at the sky and noticing clouds floating by. You don't try to change clouds when you are lying down looking up and lying here now you simply notice and accept whatever comes to your attention as it is unfolding in this moment, whether bodily sensations, thoughts, ideas, or emotions. Experience whatever comes to your attention.

Notice where your body contacts whatever is supporting you. Feel your heels, calves, thighs, legs, bottom, back, shoulders, arms, and head resting on the bed. As you become aware of lying there, notice that you are breathing.

Begin noticing what breathing feels like, the actual physical sensations of breath. Notice the rhythm of your breath, how it moves your belly and even slightly moves your chest. Sometimes I am keenly aware of my breath as it enters my nostrils—particularly when it is very cold outside. Can you become aware of your breath traveling through your nostrils, down the back of your throat and windpipe and into your lungs? Is your breath short or fast or long and deep? It doesn't matter.

Although there is no need to because we've been breathing perfectly well all day, after noticing our breath we often want to control it. Our breath doesn't need our thoughts. All you want to do is just notice how your breath is, allowing it to continue moving at its own rhythm, with its own natural movement.

Now imagine and follow the path of the oxygen delivered to your lungs as it distributed throughout your body. Imagine the oxygen path into your lungs, down your legs, into your feet, all the way to your toes. Bring your mind's eye to your toes. Can you feel your attention on your toes? Perhaps you notice a buzzing, a tingling, a warmth; perhaps pulsing, pins and needles, numbness. There's no right or wrong feeling or sensation to have. Whatever you are noticing is perfect; whatever you are noticing right now. Perhaps you are aware of nothing else besides knowing that your attention is on your toes. That is okay too, just being aware of where your attention is.

After settling your attention on your toes for a few breaths, release your attention on an exhale and move your attention to the balls of your feet. After a few breaths there, slide your attention from the balls of your feet to the soles of your feet. Then to where your heels are touching down and to your ankles.

Now move your attention to your ankles, the outer surface of skin and inner bones, muscles, tendons, and ligaments that support walking. When ready, exhale and settle your awareness up to your calves and shins for a few breaths. When you are ready move your awareness to your knees. Let your awareness circle and include the back of your legs, the kneecaps, the joints inside, and the skin around the whole circumference.

Moving from your knees, place your attention on your thighs including the body's largest muscles, the quads. From the side touching the bed around to the top facing the ceiling, the skin, muscles, bones, tendons, and ligaments. What do your thighs feel like? Anything buzzing here? Many people can feel their pulse. Can you? What does it feel like?

Exhale, and on the inhale focus your attention on your hip and pelvis, where your bottom touches the bed. Spend a few breaths sensing what it feels like to focus your attention on your pelvis, hips, and buttocks.

Exhale and place your attention on your lower back area below your rib cage, including the sides and the front. Notice the effect the movement of breath has; your belly expanding as you inhale and flattening as you exhale. Can you maintain awareness of your breathing and how it physically moves your abdomen? Can you maintain breath awareness for the complete cycle including the pauses before inhaling and before exhaling? Does the expansion and contraction of your belly affect the sensations on your skin from clothing or from pressure? And are there any internal sensations you may be experiencing right now?

Now bring your awareness higher to the diaphragm lower rib cage and middle back where some internal organs lie. If as you move through this meditation, you notice something holding your attention, imagine your breath going into that part of your body and affecting it. Allow your breath to stay and breathe at its own rhythm.

Now bring awareness to your chest and rib cage and around to where the upper back touches the mattress. Notice how the chest expands and contracts if ever slightly with each breath. Appreciate your heart and your lungs working here.

Become aware of how your shoulders and upper back may be affected by the moving breath movement. Sense where your neck joins your shoulders starting from the broad base of shoulders narrowing to the neck itself. Bringing your awareness to the movement of air happening in the neck.

Exhale and with your next breath, let your awareness flow from your shoulders down your arms all the way to the tips of your little fingers and thumbs. Imagine your breath following your attention to the fingertips as you breathe in. Now imagine the breath returning from the fingers and shift your attention as it returns to the joints of your fingers. And then to the knuckles. And then from the knuckles to the back of the hands. Then the palms of your hands. Place your attention on the to where your thumb connects to your hand. Now the side of your hand. Sense both the interior and exterior portions of your hand. Do you feel your skin and are there any sensations from within your hand?

Continue shifting your awareness up now to your wrists and lower arms all the way to your elbows. Continue gliding your focus from your elbows to your upper arms, back into the shoulders, and into the base of the neck. From the base of the neck bring your awareness up your throat to your jaw.

Now focus on sensations you may have inside your mouth. How and where is your tongue resting? What do the inside of your cheeks feel like? What about the roof of your mouth? Now your gums. And your lips, inside and out.

Now moving to the outside of your lips and to your cheeks. Become aware of your nose and nostrils. Feel the breath coming in through the nostrils and leaving. After a few breaths focus on your cheek bones, eyes, eye sockets, and eyelids.

Now your ears. What do you become aware of as you focus on your ears?

Now your entire head what do you sense when you focus on your whole head?

Finally, focus on the sense of your entire body from the top of your head to the bottom of your toes. Allow whatever sensations appear wherever. Include all body parts inside and out. Head, shoulders, arms, elbows, wrists, hands, fingers, torso, pelvis, legs, knees, ankles, feet, toes, and organs. And allow things to be just as they are, just as you find them. Now is not the time to fix or repair anything. Now is the time to see ourselves exactly as we are: whole and complete.

Walking Meditations

> *The miracle is not to walk on water. . . the miracle is to walk. . . .* —Thich Nhat Hanh

The first walking meditation I participated in was in a hotel ballroom. It was perfect! Air conditioned, carpet-cushioned, and roomy. There were only two dozen of us in a room that held 550 and most of the room was devoid of furniture, just seemingly acres of indoor turf for us to walk without fear of bumping into anyone or anything. (Come to think of it, it would have been the perfect place for students to walk and scroll through their news feeds. Windowless drab colors they wouldn't miss anyway, and nothing to trip over or smack in to.)

There are guided meditations to listen to while walking, but I prefer the silence, although sometimes I count my steps if the noise of my thoughts gets too busy. I enjoy walking meditations in nature as well, on (uncrowded) beaches—I find the surf at the beach perfect soundtrack—and in parks. I prefer to walk any clear path which is at least 15 to 30 paces long so that I am not spending all my time turning around. I usually walk with my hands at my sides, although many people feel comfortable with them clasped in front or behind their backs. Pick whichever is most comfortable for you.

The idea of a walking meditation is to focus on—you guessed it, walking! The way we focus our attention on walking is by walking. . . . V. . .e. . .r. . .y. slowwwwwwwly. Like the sloth in *Zootopia* typing or stamping papers, we want to walk at the pace of retreating icebergs.

The idea is to remain relaxed and alert, paying particular attention to sensations in your feet and legs. Do our legs feel light or heavy as we lift them? Is there tightness or tingling? Is there any pain? Notice how the sensations shift from leg to leg and from leg to heal to ankle to toe. At normal speeds walking feels as if it is one motion. Slowed down, we can appreciate the intricate differences in placing one foot down while lifting the other. Sense each step fully as you walk in a relaxed and natural way to the end of your path.

When you arrive, stop and pause for a moment. Feel your whole body standing there. After a few breaths and checking in with your whole body, slowly and intentionally turn to face in the other direction. Then pause before walking again. I use these pauses to gather myself, sometimes even closing my eyes to help me focus.

As you are walking, I promise your mind will wander. Whenever it does, before you return your attention to the sensations of walking, try to note where your mind went. At times strong thoughts, emotions, or feelings may arise as you walk. It is okay to pause when this happens. Stop in your tracks, feel the present moment, and acknowledge whatever caught your attention. Stand with it until it subsides, and then continue your walking.

You might alter your pace while you are walking, perhaps seeking a speed that maximizes your ability to be mindful of your experience. Then you can enjoy moving back and forth along your path ever arriving in the aliveness of here and now.

Informal Practices

It's All About the Pause

Informal practices, mini meditations, lightning pauses, timeouts, whatever you want to call them, are all about the pause. Opportunities to step outside of doing into being. Outside of busying into experiencing. Outside of autopiloting into piloting. Outside yesterdays and tomorrows into today. We carry with us all the tools necessary for informal practices, our breath and five senses.

We can step outside whatever current is carrying us along at any time we choose and stop to breathe. To soak in the moment. Its scents, sounds, and sights. Even if we are not eating, we can sense our mouth; is it dry or moist? And we are always touching something. When we are standing, we can always feel our feet touching the ground. When sitting or reclining we can always sense whatever is holding us up wherever our bodies are supported. We just have to think about doing it; think about taking a moment out of doing to just be. The more moments we take and the more often we take them (the more often we get to the mindfulness gym) the stronger our ability will grow to remain calmer and more poised as we navigate the maelstroms of life.

Three Breaths

Your breath is yours and always with you. Fortunately, it is ruled by the autonomic nervous system (thank you autopilot!) Unfortunately, since we don't have to think about it, we all take it for granted. It is remarkable how it delivers oxygen our trillions of cells need, and then collects and removes the trash. Incessantly. Every minute of our lives. All day and all night. I think the breath deserves a few atta-breaths now and then. So why not pause, take a few breaths, and focus on wherever you feel it in your body. It's your breath; no one can take it from you and no one can stop you from taking one or two or three.

Incorporating Moments of Mindfulness Throughout the Day

Formal meditation practices help develop the muscle of mindfulness. As I mentioned before, they are akin to going to the mindfulness gym. Sprinkling moments of mindfulness throughout your days helps as well. They are quick and also quite useful in helping you remember that you are more than whatever storm is currently brewing or blowing.

Anytime, Anywhere

Find your times and places for minibreaks. I know people who use sticky notes on mirrors, refrigerators, doors, cabinets, computer screens, office doors, and other places where they want to plant reminders. The stickies can say anything. Breathe! Stop! Pause! Wait! Time Out! Me-Hug! They can be blank; it doesn't matter because the reminder brings mindfulness to mind.

Other people I know pick times and places. You can set alarms—a beneficial use of your portal-to-anywhere-but-here! One time I regularly practice is red lights. Red traffic lights have always annoyed the snot out of me. I have long felt that the universe purposefully used its remote to bring on the yellow just to ruin my day. So evil were red lights to me that I would even purposefully change the route I was driving to circumvent them. *Oh, the light is red at my left turn. I'll just drive past it, pull a u-ey, and make a right. That way I can keep moving.* I decided to stop all that nonsense and so now I try to enjoy all my stop lights and breathe. Well, I don't actually enjoy all red lights all the time. Just today(!) I changed lanes to drive past a red light I was going to turn left at, pulled a u-ey, and made a right instead. In my defense, I knew the light is a long one and I had already mindfully waited through one cycle of lights. There were too many cars in line, and I didn't make the light. Mindfulness allows us a pause so we can determine appropriate responses instead of relying upon kneejerk reactions. So, I mindfully decided one mindful light cycle was enough for that light today.

Using the Stairs

I covered waiting for the elevator earlier, taking the stairs is healthier. One thing to keep in mind about mindfulness is to treat whatever activity you are engaged in as paramount, not as a means to an end. If all you think about while taking the stairs is getting to the top or to the bottom, then you are not being mindful *of the being of climbing or descending the stairs*. You are just on auto pilot: one foot in front of the other. You can incorporate a bit of walking meditation. Feel your legs and feet lift and come down. On the way down, feel the full weight of your body coming down on the leg on the lower step. On the way up, feel your quads in the leg on the higher step as it lifts your whole body up. Perhaps you use the handrail; feel it slipping through your hands. By climbing the stairs, you are already getting physical exercise, why not sprinkle some mindfulness exercise in too?

Washing Dishes

Whether you are a fill-the-sink, or running-water dishwasher, the goal to mindfully washing dishes is to focus on the one item in your hands instead of on the mountain remaining to be washed—especially Thanksgiving Day when the mountain is prodigious, frightening, endless, and ever growing! Use four of your senses to focus on the plate, pot, or utensil; I strongly advise against tasting it.

See each item in your hand. *Wow, grandma's good China. I remember when I wasn't big enough to be trusted washing it!* Notice how long the tines are on the forks. The different shapes of the teaspoons and tablespoons. How nasty the roasting pan is. How some food wipes off easily and other food needs a bit of elbow grease. Inspect the scrubby, washcloth, or sponge you use. Is it about time to retire it and get another? Are there soap bubbles? Watch the water cascade off whatever you are rinsing and notice how clean and wet it is now.

Feel each item, how utensils feel different than plates, plates different than drinkware, and drinkware different from pots and pans. Do you handle grandma's China differently than the knives and forks? Handle carving knives differently than the butter knives? Feel your wrists and fingers twist, rotate, and bend to work in synch? Feel the temperature of the water. Hot enough? Cold? Too hot? Feel how slippery the soap is? *Careful this is grandma's good China.*

Listen to the sounds of the running or splashing water. The sounds of clean, wet dishes piling up. The sounds of kitchen banter if others are pitching in. Or if it's not a big feast and just a few dishes, notice the general silence except for the sounds you produce at the sink. Perhaps background music filters in as you focus on the dish in your hand.

Smell the dish soap and any lingering scents left from cooking the meal. Smell the moisture surrounding you. *Ooh, is that dessert? It smells like it's ready to come out of the oven.*

Eventually the dishes will be done. And while there is satisfaction rinsing the sink and drying your hands, there was also the all the time spent away from worries and concerns one dish at a time. And someone else can take care of the dessert mess.

Brushing Your Teeth

Sounds silly, brushing my teeth? Why pay attention to brushing my teeth? What is there to notice about brushing my teeth? Squeeze some toothpaste on and brush! Oh yeah, rinse and spit.

For starters, do you floss before or after you brush? (I have had dentists who prefer flossing first, and I have had dentists who prefer flossing after. If dentists cannot figure it out, I guess it does not matter, but since you are currently focusing on brushing your teeth, which camp are you in?) Next, what about your toothbrush? Electric or manual? What color is or what colors are, your toothbrush? Are the bristles soft or hard? Are they well-worn, or maybe it is a new brush? Do you wet your toothbrush before applying toothpaste or do you just squeeze it on dry? And if you wet your brush, do you leave the water running while you brush your teeth or do you turn it off until you are done?

What brand of toothpaste do you use? Is it the same brand you used growing up? Are you a squeeze-the-tube-from-the-bottom kind of person, or do you just squeeze it anywhere? What does the toothpaste smell like? What does it taste like? Where do you start, top or bottom? Left side, or right? Some people brush their tongues and the roof of their mouths, do you? Which hand do you use? How long do you brush? (Someday treat yourself to the experience of switching hands—brushing your teeth suddenly becomes a whole new experience!)

Pay attention to your wrist. It is a virtuoso; watch it play your string of teeth as if it were holding a violinist's bow. It effortlessly changes the angles, pressure, and pace of the brush as necessary. Do you apply a lot of pressure, or do you go more softly? Do you stare at yourself in the mirror, close your eyes, or perhaps you pace as you brush?

Do you feel the brush against your gums? Do you use the same angle on all your teeth? And finally, when you are done, how do you rinse your mouth, with a glass of water, or do you cup your hands under the faucet? See? There are many things you may pay attention to while brushing your teeth instead of worrying about instead of next week's midterms.

Showering or Bathing

What a shame that most of our baths and showers are rushed affairs. I understand; time is short, and we always seem to have more to accomplish in a day than is possible, so "wasting" time washing ourselves up seems extravagant. Instead, we pretend to multitask and worry our way through our to-do lists, or about how unprepared we are for Professor Property. We think of what didn't get done yesterday or how close the paper deadline is. We focus on anything other than the task at hand.

It doesn't matter whether you are taking a long well-deserved bath or a quick shower, paying attention to bathing yourself pays dividends. Worrying about deadlines and compiling to-dos can wait (In fact with enough mindfulness practice, worries seemingly grow smaller as our perspectives change.) There is a time to plan your day and week, but not now when you are naked in the shower armed with just soap and shampoo. Just as when you are standing at the sink washing dishes, use four of your senses to focus; again, I strongly advise against tasting anything. Here we will focus on taking a shower.

Listen to how the stillness is broken as you turn on the water. What does it sound like? Notice the drain and how the water sprays from the showerhead and bounces off the walls and floor. Feel your dry feet get wet as you enter. Do you feel the water with your hand and arm and adjust the temperature to your liking before stepping under the rainfall? Is the showerhead adjustable? If so, do you like it to spray hard or soft?

Do you use body wash or a bar of soap? A washcloth, scrub brush, or scrubby? In any case, feel your hands, soap and water make their way around your body as you wash. See the bubbles? Notice the scent of your body wash; chances are its aroma had something to do with you buying it. If it is time to wash your hair, apply the shampoo, feel your fingers massage it in. Inhale deeply, what do you smell? Work up a lather and feel the bubbles. Are you a rinse and repeat kind of person? If so, what feels different about the second wash than the first?

When all the washing is done, watch the clear water roll down your body as you rinse. Notice how you turn, move, and rotate to rinse everywhere. Before turning off the water and opening the shower door, there is always time to pause for three breaths just to feel the water wash over you. You are clean.

Enjoy a Glass of Water or Cup of Coffee or Tea

Cold brewed or iced? Coffee shop or made at home? Cappuccino, Espresso, or Mocha? Paper cup, ceramic mug, or thermos? Black, sugar, cream, or froth? The options to enjoy coffee are endless and nobody has dibs on the best way to drink it.[3] Endless too, is the list of ways we interrupt what could really be a simple pleasure. The same list we use to interrupt life all the time.

[3] I learned this lesson years ago and blogged about it. See, https://mewalls.wordpress.com/2010/11/01/hello-world/.

What if instead of focusing on somewhere else or on another time, instead of compiling to-dos and reinforcing worries, what if you took a few minutes to enjoy a cup of coffee? To see, smell, taste, feel and yes, listen to it; to listen to the sounds of coffee brewing, or of the chatter of other customers, or of the idling car engines waiting in line; to look at your coffee. Is it your favorite mug or in a paper cup? What color is your coffee, and what, besides "coffee", does your coffee smell like? When you sip it, what does it taste like? Did they get your order right? swallow it down? How does the cup or mug feel in your hands? Is it too hot; need a cardboard mug wrap? Maybe it's iced and too cold. How does it feel in your mouth; do you swirl it around in your mouth a bit before swallowing? It's your cup of coffee, you can enjoy it however you'd like. The world, your worries, and your to-dos will wait.

When Called on in Class

Your palms are sweaty, your heart pounding, your breath shallow, and your muscles tense. You know Professor Gott U. Now hasn't called on you yet this semester and you fear today is the day. Now's eyes catch yours. Good thing you have been practicing mindfulness and staying in the moment for the past several weeks, otherwise you would be moments from a full-blown anxiety attack.

Now, if you happen to be right and Professor Now calls on you, you know what to do. You know to immediately accept what happened. *Yep, that's my name. Knew it.* You also know to just stop and breathe. Take a deep quiet breath (or two or three if you want). The idea is not to be theatrical but to give you pause, a place for you to focus. You know the material because you paid attention and took notes while you read it last night and you reviewed your notes this morning after you arrived early for class. You gather yourself and while you still feel your sweaty palms, your pounding heart, and your tense muscles you realize that at this distance they do not matter much, they are just noise in the background what matters is answering Professor Now and a quick look at your notes tells you that you that you've got this, that you Gott U. Now.

Stop Lights

While I covered stop lights above, I just want to add that I find them particularly useful reminders to practice mindfulness because they are naturally occurring events and because sometimes they still annoy the snot out of me. Many of my friends and colleagues use aids such as alarms and sticky notes to remind them to practice mindfulness. Stop lights are regularly and naturally occurring events which remind me that mindfulness is an ongoing practice, not a destination.

Driving Without the Radio

Most of my life I've listened to music while driving. If not the radio then I listened to 8-track and cassette tapes or CDs. The advent of iPod was magical until that ancient technology gave way to streaming. I went from listening to primarily Rock N' Roll and Jazz, to listening almost exclusively to NPR. Now I enjoy driving in silence. I enjoy experiencing the sense of the drive. I try to sink into the sights, sounds, and flow of traffic around me.

There are two times I still listen to music while driving, when music becomes an integral part of the drive. In the past, the radio was just noise. Yes, I heard songs I liked and turned the volume up and I heard interesting news stories as well. But generally the music or stories were pretty much surplusage, noise droning on in the background being ignored as the miles passed by. Sometimes, however, the music is as important as the air in the tires and gasoline in the tank—when I am driving top down to the beach with rock 'n roll blasting, and when I am driving anywhere with any of my children. As far as the former, it seems to me almost a sacrilege to head to the beach silently with the top closed and the air conditioning on. And as for the latter, each of my children are remarkable DJs and they always treat me to personalized tailer-made concerts.

Eating

Mindfully eating is taught in MBSR classes, often using a raisin. Imagine the *Zootopia* sloth again as you did above with the walking meditation. The Palouse MBSR devotes 12 minutes to eating two raisins. During the meditation first we look at, closely inspect, the raisin. Its color and wrinkles. We look for its belly button where it was once attached to a vine. We roll it around in our fingers and feel its bumpy texture. Some raisins are squishy. Some are harder. Eventually, with the pace of a sloth, we smell the raisin—I remember the first time I detected a scent from my raisin, the first time I actually smelled something! Then, yes, we bring the raisin close to our ears and try to hear it. My ears always fail me, but some students, not all, tell me they hear their raisin. Finally, we place the raisin between our front teeth—no tasting yet, just feeling the raisin between our teeth and then rolling it around in our mouths. Eventually we pierce the raisin with our teeth, and taste it until countless little bites extinguish it. Before eating the second raisin, we explore all the people and technology that were involved in getting our once upon a grapes into our mouths. We eat the second raisin more quickly, but not hastily.

Eating at sloth speed makes for an interesting lesson, however I do not recommend eating entire meals that way, just like I do not recommend always walking at the speed of walking meditations. We can walk and we can eat mindfully however, without slowing both to a crawl. Save the formal walking and eating mediations for when you are in the mindfulness gym. Outside the gym practicing mindfulness simply means paying attention to what you are doing.

If you are eating a slice of pizza, enjoy our pizza. Feel it, smell it, taste it. I am not big on listening to slices of pizza, but you might listen to whatever else is going on around you at home or in the restaurant. Another tip for eating mindfully is to put your utensils down between bites. Pay attention to each bite—not slothful attention, but notice the variety of textures, tastes, and smells.

Taking a moment to just take it all in. Whether you are at home, at a restaurant, or fast-fooding it, take a moment and realize how fortunate you are to have the time, finances, and opportunity, for this meal. And finally, if you are with someone or are enjoying the meal alone, savor the company.

PART 4

Additional Resources

People

Professor Katerina Lewinbuk

Professor Katerina Lewinbuk is a Professor of Law at South Texas College of Law Houston. Before beginning her teaching career in 2002 at the University of Illinois Chicago, Professor Lewinbuk was an associate at the Chicago, Illinois office of Baker McKenzie. Professor Lewinbuk joined the faculty of South Texas College of Law Houston in 2006 and has taught internationally and directed study abroad programs for American students. Professor Lewinbuck has long championed efforts to bring mindfulness to law school curriculum and regularly teaches mindfulness to law students. Also instrumental in initiating the annual Mindfulness Mini conferences at the Southeastern Association of Law Schools along with Professor Reuben, Professor Lewinbuk continues her work co-coordinating and presenting the programs.

Professor Richard C. Reuben

Professor Reuben is the James Lewis Parks Professor of Law at the University of Missouri-Columbia School of Law, a Senior Fellow at the law school's Center for the Study of Dispute Resolution, and Co-Director of the Center for the Study of Conflict, Law & the Media. A prolific writer, Professor Reuben has long supported efforts to bring mindfulness to law school curricula and was instrumental in initiating the annual Mindfulness Mini conferences at the meetings of the Southeastern Association of Law Schools along with Professor Katerina Lewinbuck. Professor Reuben received a grant and studied the *Efficacy of Mindfulness Meditation in the First Year of Law School to Ease Stress, Improve Performance, and Enhance Satisfaction* in 2012. He also presented *The Impact of Mindfulness Meditation Practices on a Professor Teaching Law* at the October 2010 Mindful Lawyer Conference held at the University of California, Berkeley.

Eckhart Tolle

Eckhart Tolle's works on mindfulness are renowned. In addition to his books and live programming, there are hundreds if not thousands of videos available on YouTube as Mr. Tolle masterfully discusses and parses the nuances of tapping into the power of the present moment.

Jon Kabat-Zinn

Jon Kabat-Zinn is a Professor Emeritus at the University of Massachusetts Medical School. His interest in meditation led him to study it and explore whether meditation could help improve hospital patients' quality of life by teaching them ways to reduce stress. The answer was yes. Decades later, thousands of patients worldwide have experienced reduced pain, quicker recoveries, and more positive outlooks after taking the Professor's eight-week Mindfulness-Based Stress Reduction class. To say Jon Kabat-Zinn was instrumental in bringing mindfulness to the United States is an understatement. His books and works cover the mindfulness waterfront.

The address of the Professor's website is https://jonkabat-zinn.com/; it offers guided meditations, books, and other support based on Jon Kabat-Zinn's works, as well as connections to world-wide resources to help facilitate learning and engaging in mindfulness practices.

Meditation Apps

I have no connection with any of these applications other than as a user. I list them here because I am familiar with them, I find them worthwhile, and they are available on both the App Store and Google Play.

Chopra App

Based on Deepak Chopra's wisdom and scientific research, the App provides a good array of meditations and well-being tools, tips, and practices.

Insight Timer

Insight Timer bills itself as five wellbeing apps in one including providing help with meditation, sleep, breathwork, yoga and contemplation. Calling itself the "largest free library of guided meditations on earth," Insight Timer also includes a subscription service.

JKZ Meditations

Consolidates Jon Kabat-Zinn's guided meditations with text from his books and video-recorded lectures.

Websites

Palouse Online Mindfulness-Based Stress Reduction (MBSR)

https://palousemindfulness.com/

Created by certified Mindfulness-Based Stress Reduction instructor Dave Potter, this free 8-week online full MBSR class is a gem. Potter, a retired psychotherapist with specialties in anxiety, stress, and trauma is a fully certified MBSR instructor by the University of Massachusetts Medical School who taught live, in-person MBSR classes in 2004.

Lessons include videos and readings by world-renowned teachers such as Jon Kabat-Zinn, Thich Nhat Hanh, Pema Chodron, Sylvia Boorstein, Tara Brach, Jack Kornfield, Sharon Salzberg, Kristin Neff, and Shauna Shapiro.

Mindfulness in Law Society

The Mindfulness in Law Society mission is "to enhance well-being in the legal profession by educating it about the benefits of mindfulness meditation, yoga, and other contemplative practices." https://www.mindfulnessinlawsociety.org/.

Noteworthy Books

Kabat-Zinn, Jon. *Coming to Our Senses: Healing Ourselves and the World Through Mindfulness*. Hyperion, 2006. ISBN 0-7868-8654-4.

Kabat-Zinn, Jon. *Full catastrophe living: using the wisdom of your body and mind to face stress, pain, and illness. Delta Trade Paperbacks. 1991. ISBN 0-385-30312-2.*

Kabat-Zinn, Jon. *Wherever You Go, There You Are: Mindfulness Meditation in Everyday Life*. Hyperion Books, 1994. ISBN 1-4013-0778-7.

Tolle, Eckhart. *The Power of Now: A Guide to Spiritual Enlightenment*. Namaste, 1997. ISBN 978-0-96823-640-6.

Tolle, Eckhart. *Practicing the Power of Now: Essential Teachings, Meditations, and Exercises from The Power of Now*. New World Library, 2001. ISBN 1-57731-195-7.

Noteworthy Blogs, Articles, and Reports

Lewinbuk, Katerina, P. *Lawyer Heal Thy Self: Incorporating Mindfulness Into Legal Education And Profession*. 40 *J. LEGAL PROF.* 1 (2015).

Katerina P. Lewinbuk & Christy Gilbert, Law Student Heal Thy Self: Teaching Mindfulness as a Legal Skill, 41 J. LEGAL PROF. 37 (2016).

Katerina P. Lewinbuk, Mindfulness Meditation, 78 TEX. B.J. 454 (2015).

Reuben, Richard C. *Bringing Mindfulness into the Classroom*, 61 *J. LEGAL PROF*. 674 (2012).

Reuben, Richard C. Beyond Stress Reduction: Mindfulness as a Skill for Developing Authentic Professional Identity, 89 UMKC L. REV. 669 (2021).

Reuben, Richard C. *Bringing Mindfulness Into The Classroom: Personal Journey*. *J. LEGAL ED.* 61 (2012).

Reuben, Richard C. & Sheldon, K. *Can Mindfulness Help Law Students With Stress, Focus, And Well-Being: An Empirical Study Of 1ls At Midwestern Law School*. 48 *SOUTHWESTERN L. REV*. 241 (2019).

The Depressed Lawyer: Why are so many lawyers so unhappy? Therapy Matters, Posted May 02, 2011.

Seeking Serenity: When Lawyers Go Zen, The Chart, CNN, May 11, 2011.

Vivo, Meghan. Addicted Lawyers Start as Addicted Law Students, Highlights American Bar Ass'n Comm'n on Lawyer Assistance Programs, 4 (Winter 2012), https://www.in.gov/judiciary/ijlap/files/colap-highlights-winter-2012.pdf.

Patrice, Joe. *If You're in Law School, You're Probably Depressed, Above the Law* (Jan. 15, 2015), https://abovethelaw.com/2015/01/if-youre-in-law-school-youre-probably-depressed/.

National Task Force On Lawyer Well-Being, *The Path to Lawyer Well-Being: Practical Recommendations for Positive Change* (The Task Force 2017), https://www.americanbar.org/groups/professional_responsibility/task_force_lawyer_wellbeing/.